Ecumenical Progress

Ecumenical Progress

A DECADE OF CHANGE
IN THE ECUMENICAL MOVEMENT
1961–71

Norman Goodall

London
OXFORD UNIVERSITY PRESS
1972

Oxford University Press, Ely House, London W.1

GLASGOW NEW YORK TORONTO MELBOURNE WELLINGTON
CAPE TOWN IBADAN NAIROBI DAR ES SALAAM LUSAKA ADDIS ABABA
DELHI BOMBAY CALCUTTA MADRAS KARACHI LAHORE DACCA
KUALA LUMPUR SINGAPORE HONG KONG TOKYO

ISBN 0 19 213954 1

Printed in Great Britain by
Western Printing Services Ltd, Bristol

Contents

Preface

In 1961, when the third Assembly of the World Council of Churches was in sight, the Oxford University Press was good enough to publish my book *The Ecumenical Movement: What It Is and What It Does*. Three years later a second edition was produced, with some supplementary material based on the actions of the third Assembly. A year or so ago the question of a third and revised edition was under consideration. As I studied the new material available, however, it seemed to me that more than a revision was necessary if anything like justice was to be done to the way in which the ecumenical movement has moved during the past decade. I am greatly indebted to the publishers for accepting this conclusion and making possible this new volume.

Links between this book and its predecessor will be apparent at many points. While I have concentrated on the decade 1961–71, I have included a number of references to earlier phases of the movement so that recent happenings may be seen in better perspective. The chronological table in Appendix II charts the main stages in the structural development of the ecumenical movement from the momentous World Missionary Conference at Edinburgh 1910 up to the present. Documentary appendixes to the earlier volume have proved useful, especially to students, and the present book supplements these with information complete to the date of writing. The Constitution of the World Council of Churches as here printed is the latest revision, based on a recent restructuring of the Council and the reformulation of its aims. While the material in these appendixes has been published in minutes of the Council I am not aware of any other publication which gathers together all this information in the form in which it appears in this volume.

It must always be borne in mind that the term 'ecumenical' is older than the present century, and that the essential ecumenical movement—that of bringing the 'whole inhabited world' (the *oikoumene*) into its true destiny within the purpose of God—is as old as history. Within the long story of the Christian Church both the word ecumenical and the reality signified by it have been in evidence in various ways and degrees in every age. What can be claimed for the modern phase of the movement, with its new initiative in 1910, is that after too long an acceptance of disunity as being normal there occurred a widespread reawakening to the need to recover the wholeness of the Church. This was seen to be imperative for the sake of the Church's mission in the world as well as for a true understanding of its own nature and of the Gospel entrusted to it. While the new beginning in 1910 was of special significance, not least because its primary concern was with the mission of the Church, many earlier movements had begun to break through denominational barriers and to break into the wrong kind of parochialism in the assumptions and behaviour of professing Christians. The work of the Bible Societies, the Student Christian Movements, the YMCA and YWCA, the Evangelical Alliance and the leadership of churchmen, lay and ordained, who could not rest in inherited denominational differences, all contributed to the awakening.

For some time around the 1910 period there were those who thought of 'ecumenism'—whether or not the word was then used—mainly in terms of Christian co-operation rather than of the unity of the Church. This attitude to a large extent characterized the early years of the International Missionary Council, the immediate organizational consequence of the 1910 meeting. But it was clear to many participants in the World Missionary Conference that mission and unity belonged together; hence the emergence of the Faith and Order movement. Again, in the first optimistic decade of the present century, the mission of the Church was conceived primarily as the obligation of a 'Christian' West to the 'non-Christian' lands of the Orient and Africa. The first world war shattered this assumption and the movement known as Life and Work began to correct the balance and to focus on the Church's task in society, east and west. The second world war with its even more awful disclosure of what man (especially man-in-society) is capable of, dissolved any lingering assumptions that there existed a 'Christendom' geographically locatable, and there began a new search for ways of expressing the whole Gospel to the whole world through a whole Church. It was in this setting that the International Missionary Council, originally concerned with 'foreign' missions, became integrated with the World Council of Churches which since its provisional formation in 1937 had brought together the two great international structures dealing with Faith and Order and Life and Work.

Until 1961 the World Council of Churches remained a very limited expression of the ecumenical movement because, despite its growing membership, many churches still stood apart from it. Only by this date had Eastern Orthodoxy begun to take its rightful place within the movement on a scale comparable to its strength. Certain forms of evangelicalism remained inadequately represented and the most patent lack was the aloofness of the Roman Catholic Church from the movement. As is now happily well known—and as this volume amply illustrates—this situation has been transformed during the past decade. These most welcome developments are only new beginnings, and they are taken at a time when the state of the world and the spirit of the age raise more searching questions than ever for the Church both in relation to its own nature and structure and to the truths on which it rests. While, therefore, the new beginnings are being made with thankfulness for all that they signify, the mood is not one of complacency. It is that of people still on pilgrimage towards the discovery and realization of the whole truth about life, God and man—truth that is of life and death importance to the whole inhabited world.

*   *   *

A distinguished prelate once told me that when a well-meaning friend presented him with a copy of my earlier book, his first step was to turn to the index and see whether his name appeared in it. Finding it there, he concluded that the book must be a good one. On this test many of my friends and former colleagues will conclude that this is a bad book. While I have paid my personal tribute to some of those who have gone before us into the world of light and to others who have retired from the World Council's service during the last decade, I have for the most part deliberately excluded reference to the names of the present officers and staff of the World Council, except in a brief appendix list or where I have quoted them directly. To have done otherwise would have necessitated a selectivity which might have been misunderstood. But I have all the time been conscious that the events I have narrated have depended on a host of friends and fellow-workers whose gifts and dedication have helped to make the ecumenical movement what it has become.

To this general rule I feel bound to make one exception. The decade under review marks the close of an era in the life of the World Council—its first great period under the leadership of its first General Secretary. As the decade closes a nomination committee is at work looking towards the appointment of the third in succession to this critical post. This means that the second holder of the office has carried great responsibilities within a relatively short period, in some senses an interim period. An adequate appraisal of Dr. Eugene Carson Blake's contribution to the movement cannot yet be made, but tribute can and must be paid to the courage and devotion with which in 1966 he accepted the summons to an almost impossible task and has brought to its accomplishment great gifts and far-reaching intentions. In three directions especially Dr. Blake has left his mark upon the Council, and all of these are of immense significance. First, no one has been more keenly aware of the necessity for the Church to 'resume its dialogue with the world'—to use a phrase which is amplified later in this volume. Secondly, Dr. Blake has been determined that in the composition of the Council's committees and assemblies the representation shall be truly a world representation. He has insistently pressed for measures which would help to shift the ecumenical movement from its historical western origins and provide for its direction and service through people of all races, so that in its counsels and staff there would be those who can bring in new worlds, culturally and ecclesiastically, to redress the balance of the old. Thirdly, Dr. Blake has brought his keen mind to bear on the structure of the World Council and he sees it into its new period equipped with instruments which, if their declared functions are faithfully discharged, will make it relevant to new days in the fulfilment of its original great purposes. Of such services any man might be proud; and for them, all who care about the movement will want to make due acknowledgement.

I add my grateful admission of a debt of honour to a former colleague in the World Council who has generously produced the typescript of this book. Miss Verleigh G. Cant has now added these few thousand words to the many millions which she has typed for me during the last thirty years and more. With this faithful travail she has also given invaluable help in the kind of research which such a book as this entails, and has been responsible for the compilation of the index.

Norman Goodall

Benson
Oxford
March 1972

1 A New Era for the World Council of Churches

Men and Movements

Movements and people are inseparable from one another. There is, of course, a continuity in the life of great movements which transcends periods and persons. Nevertheless the character of the movement is determined by those who serve it and whose loyalty its purposes evoke. The World Council of Churches could no doubt have come into existence through other persons than those who led it in its formative period, but in fact the Council as we now know it received its characteristic features through a particular group of men and women in whom the need and the occasion were providentially matched. 'I being in the way,' said Joseph to his brethren, 'the Lord led me.' The World Council of Churches came into existence because certain people, being in the path of his purposes, the Lord led them.

Foremost among these is the first General Secretary, whose retirement in 1966 was one of the most significant moments in this decade of change. In Willem Visser 't Hooft the hour and the man were met in signal fashion. I once asked him about his astonishing facility in the use of many languages. 'It's quite simple,' he said. 'Make sure of being born in a small country whose language no one else will trouble to learn and you will just have to do the learning.' Not only language but the literature, art, and the most significant movements of thought in other countries became native to his far-ranging mind. None of this is merely superficial. All his thinking is in fundamental terms. His manifold interests go deep and his finely tempered mind always has a disciplined sharpness about it. Had life required of him the work of a professional theologian there is little doubt that he would have been one of the foremost theologians of his day. As it is, he instinctively thinks theologically about contemporary issues in the Church and the world, combining this quality of thought with keen political perception and diplomatic sensitivity. To his twenty-eight years' service as General Secretary, first of the Council during its ten-year formative period and then following its formal inauguration in 1948, Visser 't Hooft brought a wide range of friendship across national and confessional frontiers. This had been nurtured through his earlier service in the Student Christian Movement and the Young Men's Christian Association. It had been deepened through the hazards of war and his relationship to the Christian resistance movement in Europe, and it was constantly extended and enriched through the years with the World Council. In speech, action, or silence Visser 't Hooft's judgement is unerring. As much as anything else it was confidence in Visser 't Hooft's utter reliability in his calling and task which encouraged others to give their time and energy to the ecumenical movement. This was true of older men than he, including those who had preceded him in the movements which led to the formation of the World Council, and it continued to be a powerful element in the inspirational leadership which convinced younger men that the ecumenical movement mattered supremely.

The newness of the new era in the life of the World Council of Churches is characterized in its personal terms not only by the end of Dr. Visser 't Hooft's regime; many others who left their mark on the movement have passed from the active scene during this decade of change. Some are still living in various stages of active and reflective retirement. In 1964 ill-health compelled the retirement of one of the most trusted American leaders, Dr. Roswell P. Barnes, whose wisdom and skill in negotiation were in great demand in the formative years of the World Council. In 1968 Dr. Martin Niemöller retired from the praesidium, having for many years enriched the Council through his great gifts and world-wide fame. In 1969 the two men who have given to the work of the Commission of the Churches on International Affairs since its formation in 1947 its most characteristic and colourful features—Dr. O Frederick Nolde and Sir Kenneth Grubb—retired. Such changes are in the nature of things, but they mark noticeable ends and new beginnings of great moment.

Death has brought its own great changes into the past decade. The veteran J. H. Oldham died in 1969 at the age of ninety-four. Partner with John R. Mott in the pioneer period at the end of the last century, secretary of the historic World Missionary Conference of Edinburgh 1910, and a key figure in all the successive movements which culminated in the World Council of Churches, Oldham, both formidable and lovable, was one of the truly creative minds of his generation. He embodied in his own thought and service some of the profoundest meanings of the ecumenical movement. Another layman deeply versed in theology and a man of vast erudition and acute political acumen was Hendrik Kraemer of Holland, who died in 1965. There is a phrase in one of Kraemer's great books on the relation between Christianity and other faiths which sums up his own character—'downright intrepidity and radical humility'. This was the combination of virtues which Kraemer required of the

Christian apologist in the encounter between the world's religions: downright intrepidity in affirming the uniqueness of the Christian revelation; radical humility in face of all that the other religions have to say concerning the soul of man and the ultimate mysteries. In his own personality this mighty man of valour somehow combined an inflexible will with most tender consideration for others. The Ecumenical Institute at Bossey, which represents one of the most far-reaching activities of the World Council, is only one of many monuments to his greatness. He was its founder and first Director. In Dr. Marc Boegner, who died in 1971, there passed from the scene another of the very great figures in the ecumenical movement. Elegant in bearing and speech and gracious in personal dealings, Marc Boegner was one who during the dark days of war and under the enemy occupation of his country, spoke for more than France in courageous word and action. He, too, took a leading part in the movements which prepared the way for the World Council of Churches. He was chairman of its Provisional Committee and one of the first Presidents of the Council.

In its new period the World Council is the poorer for the loss of other men at an age when much longer service would normally have been expected of them. Leslie Cooke, an Associate General Secretary of the Council and Director of the great enterprise of Christian Aid (constituting in the present structure of the Council the Division of Inter-Church Aid, Refugee and World Service) died in 1967 at the age of fifty-nine. A skilled administrator, Leslie Cooke was responsible for the enormous development of this aspect of the Council's work between the years 1955 and 1967. At the same time he gave expression to the theological and spiritual significance of all this service to human need with gifts of voice and pen inseparable from his primary calling as a minister of the Word. He was an Associate General Secretary of the Council as well as Director of its largest Division, and his death left a very noticeable gap at the heart of the administration. This kind of loss in general counsel as well as in specialized responsibilities was increased in 1967 when Philippe Maury, then the Council's Director of the Department of Information, died at the age of fifty-one. Philippe Maury, son of one of the leading pioneers in the ecumenical movement—Pastor Pierre Maury—brought to all his work an engaging personality and a mind brilliant and lucid. He was an outstanding representative of a new generation of French Protestants, *en rapport* with contemporary intellectual developments and political trends in Europe and one to whom the highest honours in any chosen profession would naturally have fallen.

Other losses have weighed heavily in this interdependence of movements and persons. Bishop Otto Dibelius of Germany, a former President of the Council and a great figure in ecclesiastical and political affairs in Europe, died in 1967. Korula Jacob of India, Secretary of the National Christian Council of India and a prominent member of several of the Council's committees, died at the early age of fifty-six in 1967. Dai Kitagawa who died in 1970 at the age of fifty-nine had brought special competence and a warm-hearted colleagueship to the Study Division of the Council, particularly in its work on the nature of Christian responsibility in a pluriform society.

Special mention must be made of two men whose unexpected death brought a particularly grievous shock to all who were aware of their unique role in the life of the World Council of Churches. On the eve of the fourth Assembly of the Council there came news of the death of Franklin Clark Fry, Chairman of the Council's Central and Executive Committees, the one upon whom the main conduct of the new Assembly in its principal sessions would have rested. Fry was President of the Lutheran Church of America and a former President of the Lutheran World Federation. He was one of the most outstanding leaders of the Church universal, whose eminence was recognized throughout the world. During the last half-century I have seen many able men exercising with great competence the mastery of assemblies. None whom I have known has surpassed Fry and scarcely any others have equalled him as a presiding officer. He was superb in his unerring judgement, in the speed and certainty of his thinking, in his control of the intricacies of debate, and his sensitiveness to all those subtle elements which affect the course of corporate discussion and resolution. These gifts in assembly were matched by a mind theologically well equipped and a standing in public life which justifiably gave him great influence in many fields of action. Fry was appointed to the first Central Committee of the Council at Amsterdam in 1948, and in 1954 he proved to be the inevitable choice as its chairman in succession to Bishop George Bell. While Fry's period of service in this office would have ended at the fourth Assembly, he was one of those men whose deep commitment to the ecumenical movement would always have been a source of strength to it.

Long before the Uppsala Assembly it had become clear that leadership and responsibility in the shaping of policy must reside increasingly in the hands of Christian leaders from Asia, Africa, and Latin America. Among the new presidents elected at Uppsala was Daniel Thambiraja Niles, a Ceylonese Methodist minister and one who for long had been a familiar and much-loved figure throughout the ecumenical movement. As a young man he had preached the opening sermon at the Council's first Assembly in 1948, and twenty years later at Uppsala he had resumed the same role when the assassination of Martin Luther King left the Assembly without its scheduled preacher. Like other ecumenical leaders 'D.T.' had served his apprenticeship in the World Student Christian Federation. As preacher and evangelist he had been in great demand in all countries. His writings, especially his expositions of Scripture, have exercised a wide and powerful influence and in the work of the World Council he had been both chairman and secretary of the Department of Evangelism. He was also chairman and secretary and, to a large extent, founder, of the East Asia Christian Conference, the first of the great regional organizations related to the World Council which are giving local expression to the ecumenical ideal. The Council was enriched by the service of many other Asians but the death of D. T. Niles in 1970 was indeed the end of an era.

World Council membership
During the past decade the increase in the number and diversity of its member churches has noticeably affected the life of the World Council. By the time of the third Assembly in 1961 the number of churches in membership had risen to 197 (at the inaugural Assembly in 1948 it was 147). Between the third and fourth Assemblies another 38 churches had joined and at the time of writing the number is about 240. Within this increase the representation of Eastern Orthodoxy has been greatly strengthened and there has been a large influx of churches from Asia and Africa. Between 1963 and 1968 twenty-one African churches and seven Orthodox churches were added to the membership. The numerical effect of this on the size and composition of Assembly and committees is some index to the spread of responsibility in the shaping of policy and the conduct of the Council's work. At the third Assembly seventy-nine delegates' places were allotted to the Orthodox churches. At the fourth Assembly the number was 161. Delegates from Asia, Africa, Latin America, and the Caribbean numbered 173 at New Delhi. At Uppsala they were 235. Assemblies are held only at five- or six-yearly intervals: while ultimate authority rests with them, it is the Central Committee, meeting annually, which carries most of the responsibility for the development of policy and the main direction of the Council's administration. A Central Committee membership of 100 in 1948 included nine Orthodox members and thirteen from Asia, Africa, Latin America and the Caribbean. In the Central Committee of 120 appointed at Uppsala twenty years later, these figures had become thirty and thirty-four respectively. Perhaps the most significant symbolic change at this point was the

election of an Asian, M. M. Thomas of India, to the chairmanship of the Central Committee.

In the earlier years of the movement it was inevitable that the World Council of Churches should bear the marks of its largely western origin. In the composition of the Assembly and its committees, and in the administrative staff, the churches of the western world made the major contribution. While an historic plea for new attitudes between the churches and for some united action had been made by the Ecumenical Patriarch of Constantinople in 1920, thus anticipating some later developments, the chief initiatives came from the European and American churches and the main burden of responsibility in support and administration was carried by them. This also meant that the theological complexion of the movement and the ecclesiastical questions with which it was concerned were to a large extent coloured by the western Protestant tradition. This generalization can be qualified by the fact that the churches of the Lutheran and Reformed traditions were far from indifferent to the historic Catholicism which they had sought to reform. Nor was Anglicanism unaffected by that type of Catholicism which the ambiguities of its *via media* permitted. Nevertheless, in the general features of the World Council's life up to the time of the second Assembly at Evanston in 1954, not only was Roman Catholicism to a large extent a marginal factor; the influence of Eastern Orthodoxy was necessarily slow in making its impact. Even when the imbalance in numerical representation is corrected, this can only be a beginning to the deeper understanding of the assumptions which differentiate the course which Christianity has taken in its eastern and western forms. In this respect it is not only the larger representation of Orthodoxy within the Council that marks a new turning point. It is the greater freedom of participation, the stronger notes of leadership in debate, and the increasing share in staff activity which are helping to make the Council more truly a world council in its character and characteristics.

A comparable process has been rapidly taking place through the role of the Asian, African, and Latin American churches in the life of the Council. While most of these churches reflect in their origin and institutional form those western denominations through whose missionary service they largely came into existence, they are rapidly moving from the position in which, except for local colour, they resemble their western counterparts. In the great matter of the nature of the Church, its ministry, its unity and the form of it, these once-called 'younger churches' provide an increasingly persistent challenge not only to the disunity of the west but to the assumption that the historic grounds for that disunity possess any contemporary relevance over large parts of the Christian world. While there is as yet in evidence little in the way of distinctive regional African or Asian theology, there is much in the contribution from these lands which raises for the west new questions about the meaning of history, the patterns of church life and the priorities in thought and action which would characterize a truly Christian community. As a result of the two factors here touched upon, the centre of gravity, so to speak, of the World Council of Churches has markedly shifted. Just as many British people, though inescapably part of Europe, find it far from easy to think and act as Europeans, so churches which by their nature and conviction are part of the Church universal may find the process of realizing their universality in the World Council one which occasions some severe growing pains and not a few nervous shocks.

The Roman Catholic Church

In many respects the most momentous development within the ecumenical movement during the decade of 1961 to 1971 is to be seen in the new attitude of the Roman Catholic Church to other churches. This has had its effect both in the relationships between the Vatican and the World Council of Churches and between Roman Catholics and members of other communions in almost every part of the world. The great turning point came with the Second Vatican Council of 1963 to 1965 and the immeasurable influence on the Council and throughout the world of Pope John XXIII. It is true that long before the Second Vatican Council the institutional impasse between Rome and other Christian communions had, to some extent, been eased by individual action and by semi-official or unofficial movements concerned with the promotion of better understanding and mutual goodwill. In the realm of personal devotion and the nurture of the life of prayer there has always been some transcending of the deepest historic differences. Hymns and prayers have largely ignored ecclesiology and there has seldom been lacking in any of the churches those who longed to see an end of disunity and whose prayers and friendship were devoted to this end. The historic initiative in the 1930s of the Abbé Couturier in widening the scope of the Octave of Prayer won an eager response. Again, collaboration in theological study, and especially in biblical scholarship, had long since created many strong personal ties. So had the widespread movement in all the churches towards liturgical study and reform. In the concern for a Christian understanding of the nature of society and of the principles which should govern international relationships, again there has been some crossing of the ecclesiastical frontiers. During the second world war, for instance, there was some joint action in Britain in the study and promotion of the principles on which a just and durable peace might be achieved after the fighting. More particularly, on the continent of Europe experience of community in persecution, suffering and resistance forged many unbreakable ties between Roman Catholics and Protestants.

All this contributed to the favourable climate in which Pope John took his momentous step. From the moment of its inception and throughout its preparation the appeal of the Second Vatican Council was to all Christians and its procedures were designed to draw representatives of all the churches into some degree of participation. The word 'observer' in relation to attendance at ecclesiastical gatherings acquired a new meaning in the generous content put into it by the Roman Catholic authorities. For the many leading representatives of other churches who more than 'observed' the proceedings things could never be the same again in their attitude to Rome, nor for the most part could the Roman Catholic members of the Council ever revert to the position which generally prevailed before this epoch-making event. The new spirit engendered by the Council continues to have its effect far beyond the life of international organizations. In cities and villages, parishes and congregations throughout the world changes in attitude, new steps in relationships, experiments in common action are in evidence. But the new chapter has also had profound consequences for the World Council itself. During its ten-year process of formation (1937 to 1948) and up to the time of its third Assembly in 1961, while individual Roman Catholics had been in unofficial touch with developments the official policy of Rome prevented anything more than this. Vatican permission could not be secured for even the most non-committal observer attendance at Amsterdam or Evanston in 1948 and 1954. Only a few weeks before the opening of the first Assembly of the World Council in 1948 a *monitum* from the Holy Office forbade all Catholic participation in the Assembly though it was intriguing to notice how many distinguished Roman Catholics remembered that they were endowed with journalistic gifts and therefore appeared in the press gallery.

For many years still the Vatican continued to issue grave warnings against participation in ecumenical gatherings, and between 1950 and 1960 a number of eminent Roman Catholic ecumenists were disciplined for ignoring the warnings. Nevertheless there were other actions which pointed in a very different direction and which show how complex the total situation was. In 1952 there was established a Catholic Conference for Ecumenical Questions. This was mainly due to the initiative of two Dutch priests, Frans Phyjeesn and Jan Willebrands. This Conference provided a regular forum for Roman Catholic theologians and from its inception it made contact with the World Council of Churches and adopted as a main item in its programme a study of the theme on which the World Council was working in preparation for its second Assembly. In 1960 for the first time there were two official Roman Catholic observers at the Council's Central Committee and at the Faith and Order Commission. One of these was this same Fr. Willebrands who, after the Vatican Council, became Secretary of the new Secretariat for Christian Unity and who, as Cardinal Willebrands, is now (1971) its Chairman. At New Delhi in 1961 Rome at last countenanced the attendance of official observers at the World Council Assembly and by this time preparations were in hand for the Vatican Council with all that it would make possible in new relationships. It was a far cry from Amsterdam 1948 to the moment when, twenty years later, there could be publicly presented to the Uppsala Assembly a warm personal greeting from His Holiness Pope Paul VI. Later chapters in this volume will reflect some of the consequences of the Vatican Council for various aspects of the work of the World Council.

In the development of organizational relationships the most important step was the decision in 1965 to create a Joint Working Group consisting of six representatives appointed by the Vatican Secretariat for the Promotion of Christian Unity and eight from the World Council of Churches. (The group was subsequently enlarged to a membership of twenty-four.) The task assigned to it was 'to work out the principles which should be observed in further collaboration and the methods which should be used'. The visit to Geneva in 1965 of Augustin Cardinal Bea, President of the Secretariat for Unity, in order to convey personally the assent of the Holy See to the establishment of this Joint Working Group was a memorable occasion, precursor of the still more significant step when Pope Paul VI visited the Ecumenical Centre in Geneva in 1969 and engaged in consultation and worship with representatives of the World Council. 'Truly a blessed encounter,' said the Pope, 'a prophetic moment, dawn of a day to come and yet awaited for centuries.' All this goes far beyond anything which could have been anticipated ten years earlier, and the rapidity and extent of collaboration between Roman Catholics and the World Council of Churches in almost every department of the Council's work gives daily evidence of progress in understanding and common purposes. It is inevitable that such steps as these should raise the question of the possible membership of the Roman Catholic Church in the World Council of Churches. In the course of his visit to Geneva in 1969, Pope Paul referred to this and said:

In fraternal frankness we do not consider that the question of the membership of the Catholic Church in the World Council is so mature that a positive answer could or should be given. The question still remains a hypothesis. It contains serious theological and pastoral implications. It thus requires profound study and commits us to a way that honesty recognizes could be long and difficult. But this does not prevent us from assuring you of our great respect and deep affection. The determination which animates us, and the principle which guides us will always be the search, filled with hope and pastoral realism, for the unity willed by Christ. We pray to the Lord that we may move forward in our effort to fulfil together our common calling to the glory of the One God, Father, Son and Holy Spirit.

This historic statement, in its caution and yet in its openness to the need for profound study of the membership question, represented also the mind of the Pope's hearers in the World Council of Churches. At the Uppsala Assembly the matter had been touched upon in connexion with the work of the Joint Working Group. The group was formally authorized by the Assembly to keep the question within its purview. In taking this action the World Council restated its basic position in the following words:

Membership depends on the initiative of individual churches willing to accept the Basis of the World Council of Churches and on the agreement of the member churches according to the Constitution. The World Council of Churches reaffirms its eagerness to extend its membership to include all those Christian churches at present outside its fellowship.

It is obvious that for the World Council itself, no less than for the Roman Catholic Church, some considerable problems—theological and practical—are involved in this question. Time is needed, not only to do justice to their depth and complexity but to make possible further growth in understanding and confidence and in practical collaboration. What characterizes the new mood is the recognition that the question of Roman Catholic membership in the Council is not foreclosed even by the most formidable historical differences and presuppositions. Nor is it only to be explored by two 'sides' in separation. There is the desire and determination to discern together the will of God for our time. Moving expression to this was given at the Uppsala Assembly by one of the Roman Catholic observers, Fr. Roberto Tucci, who said:

The Roman Church has no intention of imposing its own ecclesiology on anyone. It makes its ecclesiology clear to the other churches merely because it wants that ecclesiology to be taken seriously, to be discussed and even contested in the light of God's word, because it believes it has a special contribution to make to the ecumenical dialogue. It accepts that this dialogue should take place on an equal footing between churches which confess the same Lord, without insisting that its own ecclesiology should influence the conditions for the dialogue.

While this utterance of an accredited observer from the Roman Catholic Churches does not constitute a formal declaration of that Church's mind, it reflects an attitude and spirit now widely prevalent and is in itself symptomatic of that vastly changed atmosphere in which these relationships are now being pursued.

The Centrality of Man?

To speak of the mood of an age is to speak of something as variable as the wind. What is the span of an age? How measure and describe as a single mood the manifold currents of thought or the prevailing assumptions within a particular period of time? Yet periods do acquire some recognizable features in their distinction one from another, even though the dividing lines are difficult to trace and the definitions far from precise. The nineteen-twenties in Britain, the nineteen-thirties in Europe and America, or the post-war moods of east and west, reflect distinctive oscillations in thought and temper. The same thing can be said of the ecumenical movement, even during its brief modern history. Within the World Council of Churches itself the past decade has thrown certain concerns into such strong relief as almost to constitute a radical change in the ethos of the Council.

One of the major studies initiated by the World Council after the Uppsala Assembly became known as the Humanum Study. For the main leadership of it the Council secured the services of Canon David Jenkins, whose Bampton Lectures in 1966 bore the title 'The Glory of Man'. Canon Jenkins' first light-hearted reaction to his assignment was to say that the term 'humanum' was 'the latest code word by which people involved in the World Council of Churches avoid the questions they cannot answer and will not face by raising one more question'. Nevertheless he accepted his task, acknowledging that it 'presents an opportunity and a challenge because it indicates a need. It is about men, about us, about our losing our way and finding our way.' For some time prior to Uppsala it had been found that the work of various divisions and departments of the Council had been reaching a stage where the fundamental question 'What is man?' was constantly raising itself. The Faith and Order movement, in its origin and history, had been primarily concerned with the question 'What is the Church?' with its corollary in such subjects as ministry and sacraments, unity and authority. It had now decided, however, to undertake a study on 'Man in Nature and History'. The Department working in the area of Church and Society was engaged in a series of consultations on such topics as 'Problems of Humanization in Society in the light of current Christian and Marxist discussion', and 'The Implications for Man and Society of the contemporary scientific and technical revolution'. The Department of Studies in Mission and Evangelism was investigating 'Human Institutions in the Mission of God', while the Laity Department was wrestling with the 'Christian Implications of the Anthropological Revolution'. Many of these undertakings were channelled into a major event in 1966 when there was convened in Geneva the World Conference on Church and Society, for which elaborate preparatory work had been undertaken in three main areas: (1) Moral issues in the change from traditional to dynamic societies; (2) The social, political, and moral problems of modern industrial society; and (3) Racial and ethnic tensions in a changing world community.

In part, this Geneva conference carried into a new era the kind of concerns which, thirty years earlier, had found expression in the Oxford Conference on Church, Community, and State, but it set them in new dimensions and raised new as well as recurrent questions. The impetus of the 1966 conference, the weight of its thinking, and the urgency of its recommendations inevitably coloured the subsequent Assembly of the World Council at Uppsala, where man, his nature and needs, his relationships and destiny dominated all discussions and constituted the main patterns in which so many of the decisions of the Assembly were reached. Two illustrations of this may be drawn upon at this point. In the report of the section dealing with the Meaning and Forms of Worship there occur these words:

In worship we enter God's battle against the demonic forces of this world which alienate man from his Creator and his fellow men, which imprison him in narrow nationalism or arrogant sectarianism, which attack his life through racism or class division or oppression, famine or disease, poverty or wealth, and which drive him to cynicism, guilt and despair.

The subject allotted to another section was 'Towards New Styles of Living'. In its original formulation, the task of this section was to give guidance for a way of life which could be recognizably Christian and yet different from that of a pietistically or ecclesiastically conditioned behaviour—the way of life of a people aware of their separation from the world. The report of this section as adopted by the Assembly recognizes that 'there are various styles of Christian life' all bearing the marks of 'joy and gratitude over the possibility to be co-workers with God in a creation stirred to newness by scientific and technical inventions'. Speaking of what it means for the Christian to 'meet Jesus Christ', the report says:

In the victims of war and exploitation, in hungry children, in the prostitute seeking to be respected as a person, in the young man thirsting for knowledge—in all these we meet Jesus Christ. Where there is a living protest against selfish accumulation of wealth, where a foreigner is respected as a colleague and welcomed as a neighbour, in those who stand up for the rights of minorities—there we find ambassadors of reconciliation in our time. Whether we are rich or poor, it is in solidarity with the underprivileged that our existence acquires direction and purpose.

'Our aim', says the report, 'is freedom for human beings to live together in mutual respect.' 'Some contours of Christian styles of living' are then sketched and these are accompanied by 'Some indications for action' which read:

(a) participation in organizations of collective bargaining (trade unions, political parties, international organizations, law courts);
(b) stimulate those in authority, and the disinherited, to act (letters to members of parliament, demonstrations, strikes, peasant leagues, training and organizing of slum dwellers, teaching and preaching, protest songs);
(c) support international development and participate in nation building. Set the example as individuals and as churches (renouncement of possible careers in order to serve the needy; transfer of wealth and knowledge by an international development tax; moratorium on ostentatious church building programmes);
(d) because racism is irreconcilable with Christian faith the churches should continue to rebuke those churches which tolerate racism, and make it clear that racist churches cannot be recognized as members in good standing within the ecumenical fellowship.

All this constitutes a somewhat original appendix, say, to William Law's *Serious Call to a Devout and Holy Life* or Jeremy Taylor's *Holy Living* and *Holy Dying*. As will be seen later, there is more to be said about Uppsala and the work of its sections, but what should here be noted is the manifest tension between what several speakers in the Assembly described as the 'horizontal' and 'vertical' aspects of the Christian life and the Church's responsibility. 'How should we view the Christian Church and the World Council of Churches?' asked one of the Orthodox participants in the Assembly. 'Should they move in a vertical direction, aiming mainly in the first place at conversion, rebirth, and fulfilment of man in Christ? Or in the horizontal direction in an activist style, aiming at the curing of the evils of the world, the betterment of the conditions of human life and the creation of a normal order of things on this earth?'

Where lies the resolution of the tension between these two contrasted terms? Is there a point of intersection where alone the full meaning of the Gospel can be perceived, the true nature of the Church understood, and where the key to recurrently new styles of living may be found? It is in the search for the answer to this question that the ecumenical movement is now moving. At the end of a decade of change it would sometimes seem that the search is taking place primarily on the horizontal plane, and that for some of those engaged in it the vertical has become as problematical as the rope in the Indian rope trick. Has the upper end of the rope any security in reality? Is the rope itself an illusion, and the story that anyone has ever seen it a legend? The mood of an age is too subtle and complex a thing to yield any clear-cut description, and an analysis of it in too sharply contrasted trends may be misleading. It would certainly be an imperfect account of the present state of the ecumenical movement and of the World Council of Churches in particular to say simply that it is divided into two camps—the devotees of the vertical and the horizontal. What most people are seeking is the place of understanding (and its contemporary significance) to which the writer of the fourth Gospel points when he says 'Jesus, knowing that he was come from God and went to God, took a towel and girded himself.' Divinity most true to itself when girded for service, humanity most true to itself and to its destiny when, taking the same path, it remembers that it also comes from God and goes to God. And if, as is most certain, the road for both leads to a cross, this may be the point of intersection where alone the tension is resolved.

Ecumenical and Evangelical

It has become customary to speak of the ecumenical movement as though it were a single manifestation. It is, in fact, a complex of many influences and movements reflecting some common aims, converging on common action, and pervaded by a common spirit. Within this general community of spirit and purpose there are great differences. These appear in the meaning given to the term 'ecumenical', in the precise aims envisaged, and in the methods of achieving them. The acknowledged unity of purpose and spirit between those who represent the differences is today far more in evidence than it was even a decade ago, and if the comparison reaches back, say, to the middle of the nineteenth century the change of temper is that of an altogether different epoch. It could be claimed, for example, that the information of the Evangelical

Alliance in 1846 was an ecumenical manifestation; indeed the word 'ecumenical' was used in connexion with some of the early gatherings of the Alliance which were attended by people of many different nationalities and different denominations. In so far as the Alliance transcended some denominational barriers and crossed national frontiers, and sought a larger unity in the interests of a more faithful presentation of the Gospel to the world, its claim to be ecumenical was justified. Nevertheless, in its inception the Alliance was also a restricted and restricting movement. As one of its ardent champions declared, it represented a rallying of the faithful against the common foe of 'Popery, Puseyism and Plymouth Brethrenism'. There could be no question from this standpoint of engaging in the ecumenical quest alongside such heretics as these. Implacable hostility was called for in the interest of what was thought to be ecumenical. This spirit has not altogether disappeared. It finds expression in some fringe features of Protestantism in Northern Ireland; internationally it still rampages through an American-based organization called the International Council of Christian Churches. The technique employed by the leaders of this organization is to convene a kind of shadow assembly in the wake of the main World Council meetings, using lavish publicity to charge the Council with being manipulated by an unholy alliance of Communist and Papist plotters. These attitudes and tactics, however, are little more than a sad caricature of that evangelicalism which, whether or not it finds organized expression, represents a continuing movement concerned with the centralities of the Gospel and the safeguarding of what are felt to be the permanent spiritual gains of the Reformation. Those who from this standpoint claim the term 'evangelical' are to be found in many of the member churches of the World Council, as well as in some other churches which cannot see their way to becoming members of the Council. Notable amongst these is the great Southern Conference of Baptist Churches in the United States of America. The Evangelical Alliance in Britain and the corresponding national alliances affiliated to the World Evangelical Fellowship also represent many of these. At the same time these alliances include in their membership some who, while repudiating the views and methods represented by the International Council of Christian Churches, remain dubious about the World Council and find it impossible to associate themselves with a body in which the Eastern Orthodox Churches play a prominent role, and which is suspected of too lightly courting the goodwill of Rome.

What marks a new situation, however, is the extent to which in this evangelical world there is a growing willingness to meet in discussion those who represent a more 'catholic' churchmanship, even though any approach to agreement on fundamental differences is regarded as unlikely. In England informal discussions have taken place between individual leaders of the evangelical movement and some Roman Catholic scholars. In the United States and Europe there have been meetings in recent years between representatives of the World Council of Churches and of various organizations representing what is generally known as 'conservative evangelicalism'. Two statements indicative of the spirit in which these contacts are taking place may here be noted. In 1969 the General Secretary of the Evangelical Alliance referred in his annual report to what he called 'an alleged deficiency in our attitude to the ecumenical movement', and said:

Membership of the Alliance is, and must always be, based on one basic consideration, namely subscription to the basis of faith which includes the key evangelical doctrines. To introduce a further point into this definition, namely the question of a person's attitude to the ecumenical movement, would be going beyond what Scripture warrants and would mean that the term 'evangelical' had been given a divisive instead of re-unifying meaning among us. The Alliance will continue to stand, as it has always done, for the essential unity of the Spirit, among all those who unreservedly subscribe to the biblical faith. At other points, including the question of attitudes to the ecumenical movement, we accept one another as brethren without attempting to lay down the policies which others should follow.

In 1967 a conference of considerable importance was held at Keele University under the auspices of the Church of England Evangelical Council, the Church Pastoral Aid Society, the Fellowship of Evangelical Churchmen and the Federation of Diocesan Evangelical Unions. While primarily an Anglican gathering, there were thirty observers present from other communions, including the Roman Catholic and Eastern Orthodox Churches. In the course of the conference much was said about the necessary involvement of evangelicals in the contemporary 'ecumenical dialogue'. 'A dialogue', said the official report of the conference,

is a conversation in which each party is serious in his approach both to the subject and to the other person and desires to listen and learn as well as to speak and instruct. The initial task for divided Christians is dialogue at all levels and across all barriers. We desire to enter this ecumenical dialogue fully. We are no longer content to stand apart from those with whom we disagree. We recognize that all who 'confess the Lord Jesus Christ as God and Saviour according to the Scriptures and therefore seek to fulfil together their common calling to the glory of the one God, Father, Son and Holy Spirit' have a right to be treated as Christians and it is on this basis that we wish to talk with them.

Further expression was given to this attitude with specific reference to the Roman Catholic Church and the Orthodox Churches. On the former the report said:

We recognize that the Roman Catholic Church holds many fundamental Christian doctrines in common with ourselves. We rejoice also at signs of biblical reformation. While we could not contemplate any form of reunion with Rome as she is, we welcome the new possibilities of dialogue with her on the basis of Scripture as exemplified in the recent appointment of a team of evangelical theologians to confer with Roman theologians.

And the report added:

We welcome the increasing opportunities of conferring with the Orthodox Churches and we trust that evangelicals will be fully represented in these conversations.[1]

As the Editor of *Frontier* said of the Keele Conference:

This was a decisive step by a group who hold one of the key positions in the worldwide fellowship of evangelicals. It would be tragic if evangelical openness and generosity were met with suspicion. We need the conservative evangelicals. The balance of the Christian faith cannot be restored without them . . . Some extremely serious disagreements remain, but henceforth discussion of these can be within the Body, and that makes all the difference.[2]

World Confessionalism
When the World Council of Churches was inaugurated in 1948 there were already in existence a number of organizations variously called councils, conferences, or alliances, international in their scope, to which many of the member churches of the World Council already belonged. These were commonly known as 'World Confessional Organizations', though not all of them were composed of churches with a strictly confessional basis.[3] The strongest and most

[1] Quotations from the official report of the conference *Keele 1967: The National Evangelical Anglican Congress Statement*. Edited by Philip Crowe, London, Church Pastoral Aid Society, 1967.

[2] John Lawrence: *Frontier*, Summer 1967.

[3] The following working agreement on the use of the term 'Confessional Bodies' was recorded in 1962 by a meeting of the representatives of these organizations with officers of the World Council of Churches:
'We understand the term "confessional bodies" to mean the organizations which represent families of churches. While each of these bodies has its own specific conception of the nature of the link which binds member churches together and of its own role in the total ecumenical life of the churches, these bodies have this in common:
(a) that their member churches share together not only the general tradition which is common to all Christian churches, but also specific

highly organized of these was the Lutheran World Conference, subsequently known as the Lutheran World Federation. There were also the World Presbyterian Alliance (subsequently renamed as the World Alliance of Reformed Churches), the Baptist World Alliance, the International Congregational Council, the World Methodist Council, the Friends World Meeting, and the International Convention of the Disciples of Christ. Worldwide Anglicanism was not provided with any strictly comparable organization though recognizable ties existed between the various autonomous provinces of the Anglican communion. In 1958 the Lambeth Conference appointed an 'Executive Officer of the Anglican Communion' with an office in London and a roving commission throughout the Anglican world. Ten years later the scope of this appointment was enlarged by the next Lambeth Conference and the title of the office was restyled as that of the Secretary General of the Anglican Consultative Council. This Council represents all the provinces of the Anglican Communion and its defined responsibilities include the following: (1) to develop as far as possible agreed Anglican policies in the world mission of the Church; (2) to keep before national and regional churches the importance of the fullest possible Anglican collaboration with other Christian churches; (3) to encourage and guide Anglican participation in the ecumenical movement and the ecumenical organizations; to co-operate with the World Council of Churches and the world confessional bodies on behalf of the Anglican communion; and to make arrangements for the conduct of Pan-Anglican conversations with the Roman Catholic Church, the Orthodox Churches and other churches.

For some years annual meetings have been convened in Geneva bringing together the principal officers of all these world confessional organizations, or world families of churches as they are sometimes called. The meetings provide the opportunity for consultation between these international organizations themselves and with the officers of the World Council of Churches. Since 1968 Roman Catholic representatives have also attended the consultations. Apart from providing a useful opportunity for sharing common concerns, these annual gatherings have demonstrated the desire of the worldwide denominations to identify themselves with the ecumenical movement and to reckon with its meaning for their respective confessional traditions.

---

traditions which have grown out of the spiritual crises in the history of the Church.
(b) that they desire to render witness to specific convictions of a doctrinal or ecclesiological character which they consider to be essential for the life of the whole Church of Christ.'

In the years when the World Council of Churches was only a possibility to be considered, it was suggested that the principal member units of the Council might be these worldwide denominational structures. The proposal was, however, rejected as being likely to weaken the direct responsibility of the churches to the new movement. Around the years 1955 to 1962 there were many expressions of anxiety, vigorously voiced by some Asian Christian leaders, lest world confessionalism and the activities of these organizations should stand in the way of the ecumenical movement. Did they, in fact, reflect a kind of denominational empire-building likely to obstruct any movement which sought to lead the churches beyond denominationalism? The challenge was salutary but the fears have, in the main, proved to be unfounded, chiefly because of the intimate working relationships existing between these world families of churches and the World Council of Churches. (An incidental index to this may be seen in the fact that the offices of the majority of these organizations are in the same building as the World Council—the Ecumenical Centre in Geneva.) Further than this, there has in recent years been a growing appreciation of the constructive role which the confessional organizations can play and are seeking to play in the ecumenical movement, especially in relation to the ever-renewed debate on the nature of the Church and the full meaning of its catholicity and unity. In 1966, writing on 'The Place and Task of Confessional Families in the Ecumenical Movement' Dr. Lukas Vischer, the Director of the World Council's Faith and Order Department, asserted that both the World Council of Churches and the confessional alliances were necessary to each other at that stage in the ecumenical movement. 'The same forces', said Dr. Vischer

which welded the churches together in a universal ecumenical fellowship also led to the development of the confessional families. No matter how well the ecumenical fellowship opened new doors for witness it was nevertheless clear from the beginning that the deep differences in doctrine and order did not permit more than the formation of a provisional and imperfect fellowship. The churches' loyalty to the truth entrusted to them therefore made it necessary for them to foster fellowship with their sister churches in a particular way. . . . The confessional alliances are a result of the fact that the ecumenical movement was only partially and not completely able to bring unity to light again. As long as the deep sources of separation remained untouched the individual traditions must create separate expressions for themselves. Their separate existence is even beneficial, since it prevents the ecumenical movement from slipping into a pragmatic universalism. Their existence aids in bringing the bases of the division to the level at which they must be solved if a truly stable unity is to come about. Thus we see that the ecumenical movement (and so also the World Council) and the confessional alliances are bound up with each other to the greatest possible extent. They are related to each other and cannot exist without one another.

This approach had also found expression in 1965 when the participants in the annual consultation of officers of the confessional families went on record as saying:

(1) We believe that to think and act as if the historic confessional church families represent the only spiritual reality to be taken seriously is to live in the 'pre-ecumenical' age. In that sense the statement of a Lutheran theologian that the confessional era is at an end, is true.

(2) On the other hand, we believe that to think and act as if the fully ecumenical age had been reached, in which confessional disagreements have been overcome and in which it is possible to think only in terms of an integrated worldwide Christian community, is premature and therefore also unrealistic.

(3) It is characteristic of the present period of church history that the Church lives 'between the times', when the confessions remain the main expressions of its life, but in which these confessions have to answer the ecumenical questions: 'What is the relevance of the faith that all the confessions hold in common for their relationship to each other and for the unity and mission of the Church of Christ today?' and 'How can they express in common witness and new ecclesiastical structures the unity of Christ which exists already and for which they are responsible to our Lord for the sake of the world?'

Pending some more universal agreement than is yet in sight on the fundamental questions which have led to confessional and doctrinal differences between the churches, there remains a necessity for a diversity of approaches to the ultimate answers. What matters is that these diverse approaches shall be pursued in openness to one another and in a common commitment to him who is the way and the truth as well as the life. The ecumenical movement today is a movement as wide and purposive and as varied as this. While it remains so it will be a movement which moves.

The World Council and Mission
The oldest strand in the modern ecumenical movement is that
which is concerned with the world mission of the Church. Amongst
the precursor organizations which paved the way for the creation
of a World Council of Churches there was the International Missionary Council which was a direct consequence of the World Missionary
Conference of Edinburgh 1910. Structurally the International
Missionary Council did not become an integral part of the World
Council of Churches until 1961 but the two Councils were con-
stitutionally 'in association' with one another from 1948 onwards.
From its inception the World Council of Churches has been concerned with a right understanding of the mission of the Church and
the way towards its true fulfilment, and this concern was made explicit with the integration of the International Missionary Council
and the World Council of Churches. At that stage the functions of
the World Council, as set out in its constitution, were amplified and
amended, and these now include the following:

(a) to promote the growth of ecumenical and missionary consciousness in
    the members of all churches;
(b) to support the churches in their worldwide missionary and evangelistic
    task.

With this act of integration in 1961, the International Missionary
Council ceased to exist as a separate entity and was replaced by a
World Council Commission on World Mission and Evangelism, together with an administrative unit known as the Division of World
Mission and Evangelism. The Commission was principally composed, as was the former International Missionary Council, of representatives of national councils or conferences concerned with
missionary policy and practice, and it was designed to meet only
at five-yearly intervals. Responsibility for the ongoing work of the
Commission resides in the Division of World Mission and Evangelism with its small committee of about twenty-five members who
meet annually. The Director of the Division is an Associate General
Secretary of the World Council. The Commission met for the first
time after the integration of the two Councils at Mexico City in
1963. The place of meeting was significant for this was the first
occasion on which a world conference on the mission of the Church

had been held in Latin America under the auspices of the World Council of Churches or the former International Missionary Council. At the time of the World Missionary Conference in 1910 there was considerable discussion whether Latin America should be regarded as a legitimate 'mission field' for Protestant missions, except in regard to certain Indian or aboriginal tribes as yet untouched by the Gospel. It was argued that as Roman Catholicism was for the most part well established throughout the sub-continent, missionary activity 'from outside' would constitute an unwarranted proselytizing. It would imply the validity of efforts to convert Christian believers from one denominational allegiance to another, a practice about which there was, to say the least, considerable dubiety amongst the missions principally represented at the Edinburgh meeting.

In fact, those agencies which were attempting work in the unevangelized areas of Latin America had easily discovered that large sections of the population had remained far beyond the reach of the Roman Catholic Church, partly because of limitations placed upon that church by the governments of countries which had broken free of their colonial dependence, and partly through the inherent weakness of the church itself. Further, in many areas it was not difficult to conclude that a nominal Roman Catholicism was indistinguishable from paganism. An increasing number of missionary agencies, therefore, especially from North America, extended their work in Latin America and this, together with the results of immigration from Protestant countries, resulted in the establishment of large Protestant communities. The majority of these were the product of that more conservative evangelicalism which looked with disfavour on the ecumenical movement or was at best hesitant about co-operation with it. Another feature of Latin American Protestantism is to be seen in the phenomenal progress in these lands of Pentecostalism, a vigorous movement which until fairly recently has also stood apart from the ecumenical movement.

Few things are static in Latin America and the position thus briefly described is no longer characteristic of the situation today. Even in the earlier years of the International Missionary Council there were individual Latin Americans who played a lively, challenging, and exuberant part in its work, and the Council's membership eventually included some national Christian councils in Brazil, the River Plate, and Mexico. When the World Council of Churches came into existence in 1948, its membership included one Presbyterian and two Methodist churches in Brazil and Mexico. Twenty years later ten churches from Mexico, Brazil, the Argentine, Cuba, and Chile were in the Council's membership. These included Lutheran, Episcopal (Anglican), and Pentecostal churches.

A new feature of the Mexico meeting, in contrast to world meetings of the former International Missionary Council, was to be seen in the presence of representatives of Eastern Orthodoxy. They were there by virtue of the membership of their churches in the World Council, for the Commission on World Mission and Evangelism, being a Commission of the Council, was representative of the main communions in its membership. Orthodox participation at Mexico, however, was the result of more than a constitutional proviso. It reflected the beginnings of a new era in the relationships between Eastern Orthodoxy and the historic missionary movement of the western churches. From the early years of the nineteenth century onwards Orthodoxy had viewed western missionary activity not only with suspicion but often with intense and bitter hostility. Doctrinally and ecclesiologically this activity appeared to the Orthodox world as the aggressive expression of a Protestantism which was fundamentally heretical and dangerous. Its evangelistic concern could only be equated with proselytism and was to be resisted at all costs. Conversely, most representatives of the great missionary enterprise of the nineteenth century regarded the Orthodox churches very largely as ecclesiastical museum pieces, lacking that vital spark which produces a passionate dedication to the task of winning the world for Christ. More often than not these attitudes were based on ignorance, fostered by isolation. Nevertheless, somewhere at the heart of both false images there were facts and experiences upon which these distortions had been built.

This situation still largely prevailed when the World Council was inaugurated. Even its initial association with the International Missionary Council was regarded with disfavour by the Orthodox churches and when the proposal to integrate the two bodies was first made it met with very strong Orthodox opposition. As secretary of the Joint Committee charged with the task of working out a viable method of integration, I was deeply involved in the conversations at that time. I can vividly recall the rise in temperature of any discussion with Orthodox leaders as soon as the word 'missions' was mentioned. On the other hand, in conversation with some of the most ardent evangelical missionary leaders, enthusiasm for integrating the two organizations was reduced to freezing-point at the mention of the term 'Eastern Orthodoxy'. It has required time, patience, openness to facts, and growth in personal relationships to change this atmosphere.

The process of understanding still needs to be carried on and carried much further, but one of the great ecumenical gains of the last decade lies in the growth in understanding and mutual confidence which has already been achieved. As already indicated, the word 'proselytism' bears very vitally on this whole situation. Although there have been Orthodox misconceptions of what Protestant missions have in fact been doing, it remains true that in such areas as the Middle East the churches which are the product of western missionary activity are largely composed of converts who had nominally 'belonged' to the Orthodox churches although they had ceased to make any active profession of their faith or their ecclesiastical allegiance. It has also to be acknowledged that for many of these converts interest in an expression of faith and in a form of churchmanship other than that of Orthodoxy was aroused through the service rendered them by the western missions (education, medicine, and other social benefits), as well as by the evidence of a spiritual vitality in Protestantism which these nominal adherents to Orthodoxy had ceased to find in their traditional or inherited churchmanship.

Mission and Proselytism

In such situations as these there is clearly a very delicate and uncertain line between 'pure' evangelism with its response in personal confession of faith and a proselytism which produces a change of allegiance for reasons other than the imperative of conscience. The issue bears upon more than relationships between Eastern Orthodoxy and Protestant missions. In some form or another it is inescapable in a situation where churches of different traditions are making their witness in separation from one another. For this reason, even before the integration of the World Council of Churches and the International Missionary Council, these two bodies initiated a study called 'Christian Witness, Proselytism, and Religious Liberty'. This was an attempt to define the issues more clearly and to work towards a possible consensus of opinion and practice amongst the member churches of the World Council. The Council cannot, of course, prescribe rules of behaviour for its member churches. What it seeks to do in matters vital to the churches' witness and to their relationships with one another is to provoke discussion at the points where responsibility rests and to bring within the discussion those whose interests and tasks are most affected. In this instance, successive drafts of the points at issue and of the way in which the differences might be resolved were made the basis of correspondence and consultation throughout the world, with the result that the third Assembly of the World Council adopted a statement on 'Christian Witness, Proselytism, and Religious Liberty in the setting of the World Council of Churches', commending it to the member churches and the missionary agencies. The statement affirmed the responsibility of every church to evangelize and its freedom to do so, though in respect of this freedom it says, 'Liberty is not absolute, for it must not be exercised in such a way as to impair the golden rule.' With this proviso the document affirms that:

Witness in word and deed is the essential mission and responsibility of every Christian and of every church. . . . Such an act of witness seeks a response which contributes to the upbuilding of the fellowship of those who acknowledge the Lordship of Christ. A person enters that fellowship by becoming a member of one of the several existing ecclesiastical communities. Both witness and response must therefore of necessity take place within the existing situation of division in the Church.

The statement then recognizes the nature of the difficulties which have occurred in the history of evangelism and declares that this essential evangelizing obedience of every church becomes corrupted when 'we put the success of our church before the honour of Christ; when we commit the dishonesty of comparing the *ideal* of our own Church with the *actual achievement* of another; when we seek to advance our own cause by bearing false witness against another church; when corporate self-seeking replaces love for every individual soul. . . . It is very easy to recognize these faults and sins in others; it is necessary to acknowledge that we are all liable to fall into one or other of them ourselves.'

The churches were then asked to accept as binding upon themselves a number of principles which should govern the practice of evangelism in liberty. It was urged:

That we in our churches respect the convictions of other churches whose conception and practice of church membership differs from our own and consider it our Christian duty to pray for one another and to help each other rise above our respective shortcomings through frank theological interchange, experiences of common worship and concrete acts of mutual service; and that we recognize it as our obligation, when in exceptional cases private or public criticism of another church seems to be required of us, first to examine ourselves and always speak the truth in love and to the edification of the churches;

that we recognize it as the primary duty of every awakened Christian to strive prayerfully for the renewal of that church of which he is a member;

that we recognize the right of the mature individual to change his church allegiance if he becomes convinced that such change of allegiance is God's will for him;

that since grave obstacles to brotherly relationships between churches are created when some churches are denied the religious liberty which is accorded to others, all Christians should work towards the establishing and maintenance of religious liberty for all churches and all their members in every land;

that while it is proper for churches to make clear their position with regard to marriage between persons belonging to different communions, the conscientious decision of marriage partners as to their future church allegiance should be respected;

that before a young child is received into the membership of a church other than that of the present affiliation of the parents or guardian, a due pastoral concern for the unity of the family should be exercised; and where the proposed change of affiliation is contrary to the desire of those directly responsible for the child's nurture and upbringing, he (or she) should not be received into membership of the other church unless there be reasons of exceptional weight;

that due pastoral care should be exercised before receiving anyone into the membership of a church if he is already a member of another church under discipline by that church, or if there is evidence that his reasons for seeking membership in a different church are worldly or unworthy;

that whenever a member of one church desires to be received into the membership of another church, direct consultation should be sought between the churches concerned; but if conscientious motives and sound reasons are apparent, no obstacle should be placed in the way of such change of membership before or after its accomplishment;

that while there may be situations where a church already present in a given area seems to be so inadequate in its witness to Christ as to call for more faithful witness and proclamation of the Gospel to its members, the first effort of other churches should be patiently to help that church towards its renewal and the strengthening of its own witness and ministry. . . .

In 1970 the discussion of this matter reached a new stage when the Joint Working Group between the Vatican and the World Council of Churches commended to both bodies a statement on 'Common Witness and Proselytism' which had been prepared by a Joint Theological Commission. This document sought to go beyond framing principles of accommodation between churches which would nevertheless still pursue their evangelistic task in complete separation from one another. Here the emphasis was on *common* witness, described as 'the witness which the churches, even while separated, bear together, especially by joint efforts, by manifesting before men whatever divine gifts of truth and life they already share in common'. 'Christians cannot remain divided in their witness', said the statement. 'Any situations where contact and cooperation between churches are refused must be regarded as abnormal.' The document recognizes that the ultimate aim must envisage a unity more complete than the common witness of divided churches, for 'the more the need of common witness is grasped, the more apparent does it become that there is need to find complete agreement on faith—one of the essential purposes of the ecumenical movement'. Nevertheless, since the burden of their common witness and the central task of the churches is 'simply to proclaim the saving deeds of God . . . what unites them is enough to enable them in large measure to speak as one'. The statement then suggests guiding principles, largely in line with those proposed in the earlier document of the World Council of Churches, by which misunderstanding—especially in situations where the danger or fear of proselytism might arise—could be avoided. The Central Committee meeting of the World Council in 1971 welcomed 'the degree of mutual understanding in an area of great delicacy' revealed in this statement and urged that it should be studied by the churches together in particular areas.

All this can only constitute an interim policy on the way towards the achievement of full unity in witness. Nevertheless, even as one step towards this end it implies certain acceptances and attitudes—in some respects radical changes of attitude—which could mark a great advance in the furtherance of the world mission of the Church.

Christianity and other Faiths

The word 'proselytism' is an index to more than a domestic issue for separated churches. It raises questions not only about the attitude of churches to one another in the pursuit of their common witnessing responsibility but about the relationship between Christianity and other religions. It concerns the attitude of Christian churches to the devotees of Hinduism, Buddhism, Islam, and the rest. In the World Council study the conjunction of the terms 'Christian witness', 'proselytism', and 'religious liberty' is important. If proselytism signifies the use of unfair means of persuasion and reflects a pride and aggressiveness out of keeping with Christian standards, it must clearly be repudiated. This being accepted, what forms of Christian witness are valid, authenticated by the nature of the Gospel—indeed, made imperative by the Christian understanding of God and man? What are the liberties which can rightly be claimed and honourably exercised in the interests of such witness?

These issues have been central to the missionary movement throughout its history. While missions have of necessity become involved in an infinite variety of activities, they have known that their crucial task has been on the frontier between the Christian faith

and other interpretations of the meaning of things. Today this
frontier has shown itself to be more formidable than it was assumed
to be a few decades ago. Islam continues to make headway in
Africa and is as deeply entrenched as ever in the Middle East. In
India, orthodox Hinduism, whether in its classic forms or popular
observances, holds its own, while a reformed Hinduism—part philosophy, part a cultural ethos, partly a deep religious conviction—
makes a contemporary appeal to a new generation. Buddhism in
Asia, which D. T. Niles once described as a religion which takes
the death of God seriously, is engaged in a world Buddhist movement and claims converts in Europe and America. Those English
Buddhists who display their ritual dances on the main shopping
streets of London and invite inquiries from the passers-by do so
in the conviction that the disillusioned heart of western man, whose
coming of age has brought so much sorrow and bewilderment, is
now ready for the tranquillity and joy which the way of the Buddha
can offer. Opinions continue to differ as to the extent to which the
present-day resurgence of the great non-Christian religions is fundamentally a religious phenomenon to be reckoned with theologically
and spiritually. The resurgence coincides with the rebirth of
nationalism, the achievement of political independence, and the
renaissance of ancient cultures in conjunction with these things.
But whatever the complete diagnosis may be, the strength and
character of the non-Christian religions has to be taken seriously.
Hendrik Kraemer and others have contended, in fact, that the contemporary encounter between Christianity and Islam, Christianity
and Hinduism, Christianity and Buddhism makes demands more
searching and exacting for the Christian at the central point of 'what
we believe' than at any previous stage in the history of the Christian
mission.

It is interesting to recall the changes which over the years have
affected the policy of Christian missions in relation to the other
religions. Such changes are never clear-cut steps; they are gradual
transitions. If to some extent we can identify periods with characteristic emphases, it has always to be remembered that the lines are
blurred. The dominant views of one period may have been anticipated in an earlier day, or may be repeated in a later situation.
There was, for example, an early stage in which the dominant emphasis was on the darkness, idolatry, and devil-originating character
of the non-Christian religions. This found support in the association
with religion of such repellent practices as infanticide, widow burnings, ritual murders, temple prostitution, and the like. The moral
revulsion was understandable, but judgement might well have been
tempered with the remembrance of witch hunts and burnings and

the branding of adulteresses in allegedly Christian societies, not to
mention tortures and deaths within the household of faith in the
name of one alleged orthodoxy or another. In this earlier period the
prevailing missionary attitude to the non-Christian religions was one
of condemnation and disdain. Yet even alongside these prevalent
tones there were Christian scholars translating and commenting
upon the classical writings of other faiths with sympathy more than
contempt.

A very different atmosphere pervaded the later period when J. N.
Farquhar's book *The Crown of Hinduism* gave a new direction to
much missionary thinking. Farquhar was a sympathetic student of
Hinduism and a good missionary to the Indian student world. He
wrote appreciatively of Indian life and especially of India's religious
quest, and he championed the thesis that Christ came to fulfil all
such quests. Christ was to be presented as the crown of the non-
Christian religions. This attitude was to some extent reflected in a
hymn of George Matheson's which could be relied upon to appear
in the order of service at most missionary meetings over a period
of about twenty years:

> Gather us in, thou love that fillest all,
> Gather our rival faiths within thy fold.

An age more sensitive to the syncretistic dangers of even a crown of
Hinduism thesis has declined to gather this hymn into most later
collections. Theologically its omission may be a good thing but I
retain an unashamed regard for some of its skilful epitomizing in
verse:

> Thine is the Roman's strength without his pride,
> Thine is the Greek's glad world without its graves,
> Thine is Judea's law with love beside,
> The truth that censures and the grace that saves.

All this reflects a mood and a period which could not survive the
Barthian age and which was bound to wilt before the stand-no-non-
sense mind of a Hendrik Kraemer. Kraemer's main contention was
that the revelation of God in Christ is fundamentally different
from—wholly other than—anything contained in the historic non-
Christian religions; radically different also from much of the reli-
giousness which has accrued to Christianity, especially in its quasi-
philosophical and institutional form. He affirmed that there are
no 'points of contact' with the non-Christian religions. What
had been thought to be such can at best only be regarded as
points of departure. Kraemer could approve what he later recognized
in Farquhar as 'a genuine desire to break with the attitude of im-
patient scorn and exchange it for that of generous appreciation' but

the crown of Hinduism theory was too facile. For the Hindu craving for escape from *samsara*, Christ offers not a culminating way of escape but a new life, quickening hopes not felt or imagined before, and kindling some of the deepest and most persistent longings of man.

For some it seemed as though Kraemer was redrawing the old battle lines between Christianity and the non-Christian religions and doing so with remorseless rigour and even a harsh insensitiveness to the poignant tale of man's quest for God. But this was to misunderstand Kraemer, the man and the missionary. However he may have appeared in some of his bludgeoning prose, as a missionary in Indonesia and in all his subsequent wide-ranging contacts, few men could excel him not only in his knowledge of the history, the sacred books, the doctrines and characteristic practices of the non-Christian religions, but in his swift and deep spiritual *rapport* with men of other faiths.

Kraemer's position, even with such modifications as he conceded in his later years, has continued to meet with challenges from men with a right to speak with him on his own ground. One of these was an Indian, Paul Devanandan, whose early death was a sad loss to Christian scholarship and the Church universal. Another is Kenneth Cragg, one of the most erudite and spiritually sensitive of students of Islam. In neither of these men could there be any dubiety about the uniqueness of Christ, his person and his saving work. Neither of them has been in any doubt about the moment when a point of contact has to become a point of departure. Yet both have been more inclined to acknowledge that this paradoxical point of contact–departure in relation to the Christian revelation would not have appeared in the religious history of mankind or in the heart of pagan secular man if God had not made available to humanity a light which lighteth every man coming into the world.

When the World Council's Commission on World Mission and Evangelism met in Mexico in 1963, the word 'dialogue' had come to be regarded as a key to the right form of Christian witness to men of other faiths. The tendency, not least in the World Council, to fasten upon a particular word for a particular occasion and then work it to death has affected the use of the word 'dialogue', but before it is superseded by another verbal fashion its importance should not be overlooked. It is intended to point to something deeper than conversation and different from argument though it may include both these things. It sees the interchange of words between persons as being set in a relationship of fundamental sympathy, of a deep desire for mutual understanding and an openness to mutual correction. The parties to such dialogue, while being faithful to their own convictions and desirous of commending them to others, together seek humbly for that insight which will lead both into fuller apprehension of the truth. Theology does not cease to be important in this. Scholarship still needs to provide its own distinctive aids. Testimony to truths inherited, whether in Scripture or tradition, assertions regarding the significance of experience, data which formed part of an earlier Christian 'apologetic' or the study of 'comparative religion'—all these things continue to have their place, but they are drawn upon within this new depth of communication arising out of a new depth of personal relationship. It is from this standpoint that the policies and programmes of the World Council are now being carried out in relation to the other great religions of mankind. Much of the work is pursued in study centres which, during the last twenty years and especially the last decade, have come into existence in various parts of the world. Some of these are the result of independent local action. Others have been due to initiatives taken by the World Council of Churches or the earlier International Missionary Council. The work of the centres is related to an overall policy worked out at such meetings as that at Mexico. These centres include the Christian Institute for the Study of Religion and Society, Bangalore, South India; the Christian Study Centre of Chinese Religion and Culture in Hong Kong; the Centre of Christian Studies in Montevideo, Uruguay; and the Henry Martyn Institute of Islamic Studies, Pakistan. There is no single study centre for the whole of Africa but work towards the same end is being done in Ghana, Nigeria, Cameroun, Tanganyika, Kenya, and Morocco. All this is related through the World Council to comparable undertakings in other lands. While focusing on the study of a particular religion and its relation to Christianity, the centres provide a meeting point between Christians and the representatives of the other faiths.

While the 'dialogue' principle implies an attitude to other religions very different from that of hostility, condemnation or disdain, it must clearly be distinguished from syncretism—an attempt to merge elements of different religions in a composite faith. It is not the equivalent, either, of an inter-faith movement which aims at the closest possible collaboration between those who continue to adhere to their separate faiths. By its very nature Christianity contains within itself a universal claim and offers a universal gift. Both claim and gift are based on specific evidence in history. The Christian believes that Christianity is good news, saving news for all mankind, self-authenticating in its ultimate convincing and converting power. Whatever part the diverse religious beliefs and practices of mankind may have been intended to play in man's search for God and God's search for man, Christian witness—whether through dialogue or other means—is witness to a Name which is above every name. This position was clearly asserted in the discussions at Mexico. Bishop Sabapathy Kulandran of the Jaffna Diocese of the Church of South India, after pointing out that dialogue presupposes an initial agreement to 'a quest common to both parties', went on to say:

But to stop with that initial agreement is to eliminate dialogue and live in the illusion that there are no disagreements. Disagreements do exist; and hence the need for dialogue. Disagreements must be faced and the greater the knowledge of other faiths the greater the knowledge of what these disagreements really are. . . . To stop at disagreements is to lose faith in the possibility of evangelism. The step from the state of disagreement to that of ultimate agreement is the most important step in a dialogue and the most important act in evangelism; it is to convince the man with views so different from ours that God's offer is being made to him also. Since all men belong to God and the commission to evangelize is to evangelize all men that step must be taken.

In the same debate Bishop Heinrich Meyer of the Evangelical Church in Germany put the issue in more passionate terms:

Our belief in Christ Jesus is at the same time the force driving us to seek and to love other men and the dividing line between them and us. . . . We know that the people holding another faith are created by God like us. God's mercy nourishes and preserves them as much as us. We know that Christ Jesus died to free them too, that their freedom is at hand, that they too are reconciled to God. We know that the living Lord through his Spirit seeks them, speaks to them, wishes to evoke faith in them too. When we meet them, serve them, love them, we meet and serve Jesus who loves them and is with them. . . . There is no value in attacking their faith and condemning it, quite apart from the fact that we are not called to be their judges here on earth. There is no value either in telling them what we find to be beautiful in their religion, apart again from the fact that we are not called to be examiners of their faith, passing notes of praise or disapproval. There is just one possibility left: to tell them as humanly and as humbly, as lovingly and earnestly as possible about the Triune God, their Creator, their Saviour and their Lord—like beggars who tell other beggars where bread can be had freely, like patients who tell other sick people where they can find the right doctor, like ex-convicts who tell other delinquents about the judge who pays the fine himself and lets the delinquents go free. Shame upon us if we the beggars, the patients, the ex-convicts do not speak of Jesus and nothing but Jesus when meeting men of other faiths and of no faith at all. Shame upon us if we did not do everything, sacrifice everything, to win them for Christ, not by force but by the all-conquering, humble love of Jesus.

The new approach to the men of other faiths is new in its spirit and methods, not in its ultimate purpose. As the constitution of the Commission on World Mission and Evangelism puts it, it is the aim of this Commission of the World Council 'to further the proclamation to the whole world of the Gospel of Jesus Christ to the end that all men may believe in him and be saved'.

Mission and the Secular

While organized religion, whether embodied in the institutions, doctrines, and practices of Christianity or of other faiths, has by no means disappeared from the world, for a great number of people in all lands the contemporary question is not 'Which religion?' but 'Why religion at all?' This applies to more than the Communist world, which answers the question with its own fundamental negation. It is a worldwide characteristic of the times, closely related to the phenomenally rapid advance throughout the world of the process known as secularization.

In 1929 the International Missionary Council, through its meeting in Jerusalem, had brought the word 'secularism' into prominence in connexion with the changes then affecting the Christian mission. In earlier meetings of the International Missionary Council, as in the assumptions of the missionary forces in general, it could be taken for granted that the strongest centres of resistance to the Christian view of man and his destiny lay in the historic non-Christian religions. By 1928, midway between two world wars, it was a secularist temper which was felt to be the most potent corrosive force assailing all religion, Christian and non-Christian. This was the burden of the Jerusalem meeting. This did not signify that the International Missionary Council then regarded secular progress as in itself inimical to the Gospel. 'We claim for Christ', said the report of the meeting, 'the labours of scientists and artists. We recognize their service to his cause in dispersing the darkness of ignorance, superstition and vulgarity. We appreciate the noble elements that are found in nationalist movements and in patriotism, the loyalty, self-devotion and idealism which love of a country can inspire.' But these secularities, so the Jerusalem meeting contended, even at their best needed to be 'consecrated', 'dedicated' to the service of the Kingdom. It was as though the missionary attitude to the secular was to take what it could out of it and harness it to the Christian cause, especially to the service and task of the Church. This almost recalled the mood of an earlier day in which, out of music thought to be sensuous and secular, the good Christian would select melodies sufficiently sober to be 'dedicated' and marked *andante religioso*.

During the last twenty years Christian theologians have tended to take a very different view from this of the real meaning of the secular world. More and more it is being seen as the sphere in which God himself is at work. The Christian does not consecrate or sanctify it; he learns to perceive God's presence in it. If we fail to look for his presence and to discern his purpose in the secular world we may lose our way in it; we may misuse its powers and wander further away from God. Nevertheless it is within the secular that we may also find him. As the report of the Commission on World Mission and Evangelism at Mexico in 1963 said:

Secularization opens up possibilities of new freedom and of new enslavement for men. We have no doubt that it is creating a world in which it is easy to forget God, to give up all traditional religious practices and at the same time to lose all sense of purpose in life. Yet we are overwhelmingly convinced that it is not the mission of the Church to look for the dark side and to offer the Gospel as an antidote to disillusionment. We believe that at this moment our churches need encouragement to get into the struggle, far more than they need to be primed with warnings. . . .

We believe that our own churches in many situations have been secularized in a bad sense; that is to say, that they have become a compartment of life, apart from the rest, and have very often submitted to making the best of this. . . . We believe that what cannot be assumed cannot be redeemed; that as our Lord took on flesh, so he calls the church to take on the secular world. . . .

The pattern of Christian mission in the secular world must be one of constant encounter with the real needs of our age. Its form must be that of using dialogue, using contemporary language and modes of thought, learning from the scientific and sociological categories, and meeting people in their own situations. . . .

The Christian message to men is not only concerned with individuals but also with the Kingdom of God as the destiny of mankind as a whole. Being released from a selfish life, we can so use the gifts of God which he has given us in the process of secularization as that we do not victimize ourselves and others. Technical skills, scientific knowledge, the time of leisure, and the power of structures receive their meaning in the service of others. . . .

The Christian message to men in the secular world does not call them into exclusive minorities, but to be the first-fruits, those who live a life of witness and service for the total community, thus forming the nucleus of the household of God in each land and among every group of people. . . .[1]

[1] See *Witness in Six Continents*, edited by R. K. Orchard, London, Edinburgh House, 1964.

'As our lord took on flesh so he calls his Church to take on the secular world.' What does this mean in practice? What does it signify for the policy and programmes of the churches' missionary agencies, and in the missionary obedience of the churches' members? The Mexico meeting could give no comprehensive and detailed answer to this question. What it mainly sought to do was to press the question home on all the churches, to ensure its serious consideration across national and denominational frontiers. Much of the present work of the Commission on World Mission and Evangelism is still concerned with this task and with finding ways and means of helping the churches to work out answers which in any given situation will prove relevant and fruitful. In this process the word 'solidarity' is being called upon to give as much overtime service as the word 'dialogue'. A missionary church is one which shows its solidarity with the neighbourhood, with the society or the nation in which it is placed. A church member alert to the missionary nature of Christian discipleship is similarly concerned to fulfil the requirements of solidarity with the community in which he lives and works. For many Asians and Africans present at Mexico this implied solidarity with their brethren in their political and social aspirations and struggles. There could be no withdrawal for Christians from a social revolution which, whatever its dangers, was bent on achieving freedom and fullness of living for those hitherto denied these things. C. H. Hwang, at that time Principal of the Tainan Theological College in Formosa, gave powerful expression to this:

Political revolution, social revolution, industrial revolution, rising hopes and new despairs—all these struggle round the Asian man and inside him. How is the Church, the first fruit of the new creation, to be related to this struggle? Is not its task to be in the struggle with a vocation to share the turmoil, for only as this turmoil is seen through Christ's eyes and only as Christ is so revealed as its answer, can the Church fulfil its mission and the nations be blessed? . . . This is a time when men, consciously or unconsciously, are crying out of the deep and crying out for the depth. It is a time when deep encounters deep. . . . The churches in these nations must be drawn into these depths, called there by God that they might rediscover their own depth and find anew their own unshakable foundation. The call is *ad fontes*. In this encounter we can only be reaching the living God, at the frontier of depth where he is reaching out to us, namely in the decisive event of nation-building, in confrontation with the social revolution, and above all in the encounter with the dying and renewing of indigenous cultures, and through redemptive wrestling with the non-Christian religions. There is real danger that we may lose our bearings as we are involved in all these but there is an even greater danger that we may not meet the living Lord if we are unwilling to go

'outside the camp' for it was there that he was crucified and rose again.
If we refuse to go outside the wall we shall become a ghetto, irrelevant
and unrelated to Asia today and tomorrow, and we shall eventually become a museum piece, a relic left over from the colonial era.

For many Americans the call for solidarity was seen as a summons
to become involved in the agitations and campaigns, the freedom
marches and all the other struggles to secure social and racial
justice. For others again, solidarity meant the fullest possible involvement in the new technological societies, especially in the demands
and dangers of the modern city—the new megalopolis. Another
speaker at Mexico, George E. Todd, Director of the Urban Church
Department of the United Presbyterian Church in the U.S.A., said:

The biblical vision of man's future is not restoration to a garden but fulfilment in a city. Man's destiny is seen to be the abundant life, fulfilled in
the meeting of men of all nations in a city. The kings of the earth do
bring the glory and honour of the nations into it. The Revelation of John
describes the skyline in detail. Not rough stones and ore of primeval
nature but cut and polished jewels and refined gold are the building
materials. The details may sound rather gaudy for modern tastes but the
picture is of an architecture raised to glorify God and to provide spacious
mansions for the inhabitants. In this vision we learn that the saints are
destined to become urban men.

Quoting David Barry, Director of New York City Mission Society,
Todd continued:

It is possible that the best contribution the urban churches could make is
to try to state as precisely as possible what they understand God's purpose to be for the urban centres in which they minister.

Applying this to New York, Todd quoted Barry as saying:

God is trying to show us that people of all nations can live together not
only in mutual respect but in mutual enrichment. He wants us to discover
that by appropriate division of labour, training and specialization the
individual's talents and powers can be released for undreamed of accom-
plishments; that this metropolitan structure can produce a wonderful variety
and diversity. He is helping men in cities to learn that the imaginative
use of finance can be a tremendous boon to humanity. He is telling us
things about the flowering of the human spirit in art, literature and culture. He is providing a theatre for all the governments of the planet to
work together for mankind's release from all kinds of bondage. He is
providing a gateway to new dignity for minority groups. All these and
much more are part of God's plan for this city.

Thus at Mexico speakers from east and west, in their endeavour to
restate the full scope of the Christian mission, were affirming that
missionary obedience requires this solidarity with the contemporary,

the identification of the Christian with movements, trends, and developments characteristic of a revolutionary period in the world's history. As an Indonesian Christian, T. B. Simatupang, put it, 'Christians are part of the crew of the revolution's vessel.'

A decade before the World Missionary Conference at Edinburgh in 1910 there was held in New York what was described as an Ecumenical Conference on Foreign Missions. In the course of its deliberations a speaker from India said 'Necessity alone will lead a missionary to interfere in secular affairs.' The speaker's immediate reference was to the needs of the hungry. 'We cannot', he said, 'expect people with empty stomachs to sit at the feet of Christ.' But the speaker and those who met in New York at that time were concerned not only with India's poverty and hunger but with a caste system which placed unequal burdens upon its lowest members. The situation called for 'interference' in the secular. This is only one illustration of the long involvement of Christian missions in the social needs of the lands in which they have served. The vast development in the nineteenth and twentieth centuries of educational and medical missions, agricultural and industrial missions, experiments in co-operative marketing and banking, all stemmed from this recognition of the necessity to 'interfere'. Often this went beyond ameliorative and social service and impinged on political issues in the identification or 'solidarity' of missions with measures of social reform. There are island communities in the South Pacific whose political constitutions and legal structures bear the marks of missionary involvement in the making of them.

Nevertheless there is a difference between this historic involvement of missions in secular affairs and the new relationship between Christianity and the secular as envisaged at Mexico and much more fully elaborated through the work of other Divisions of the World Council and expounded at the Uppsala Assembly in 1968. What is this difference? It lies in the difference between approaching the secular from outside in order to change or challenge it and learning from the inside its meaning and possibilities. Missions have always acted in the conviction that the Church is *sent to* the secular with news about God, man, history, and destiny. Yet being *sent to* suggests an initial separation *from*. In the new emphasis the movement is from within the secular as a realm which is itself created by God, within which his presence is to be discovered and his redemptive work realized. In such an emphasis there is the obvious danger that all distinctions may become blurred between the secular as it now is and as it is meant to be and to become in the purpose of God. Therefore, however vital the current emphasis may be on solidarity, it is still necessary to ask: 'Is solidarity the beginning and end of mission?' R. K. Orchard, writing from the standpoint of one long involved in the work of the World Council's Commission on World Mission and Evangelism, has said:

Solidarity by itself is no more the right relationship with the life of this present age than was isolation from it. Some whose rightful concern is to bridge the gulf between the churches and the daily life of men sometimes seem to suggest that by identifying ourselves with our fellow men in their hopes and needs and sorrows, by entering into the estrangement of contemporary man, we shall thereby discover Jesus Christ. This is a dangerously misleading way of stating the matter. It is true that we shall not discover or live with Jesus Christ without entering into a genuine relationship with our fellows in their needs and sorrows, that the philosophy of 'I'm all right, Jack' in whatever sphere it appears—religious, social, economic or political—is the antithesis of the Christian Gospel, but to suggest that by identifying ourselves with our fellow men we shall discover Jesus Christ is just plainly false. It ignores the fact that Jesus Christ did not only identify himself with men's hopes and needs and sorrows. He dealt with them in both judgement and mercy, and in dealing with them he not only was at one with men in the incarnation but also separate from them in the ultimate separation of the crucifixion. So those who participate in the Event of Jesus Christ are called both to solidarity with their fellow men and separation from them, and both the solidarity and the separation are 'in Christ'.[2]

This sounds a note similar to that voiced by one of the participants in the National Evangelical Anglican Congress at Keele in 1967. J. N. D. Anderson, writing on 'Christian Worldliness', admitted that 'Evangelicals, pietists and monastics have frequently held an unbiblical doctrine of separation from the world . . . and a naïve belief that withdrawal from the world would mean an emancipation from evil.' Nevertheless, accepting as an Evangelical the necessity for a new view of the secular, Anderson went on to criticize 'contemporary voices' which 'have advocated an exaggerated doctrine of assimilation to the world'. 'The biblical position', he added, 'is that we should be equally involved in the world and yet separate from it.'

Mission to Six Continents

The main shift of emphasis illustrated at Mexico carried with it new or renewed insights into the nature of the Church's missionary task. The title which the Commission at Mexico gave to its published report was 'Mission to Six Continents'. This was intended to challenge more radically than hitherto any assumption that the western world no longer itself needed to be evangelized. No part of the world is simply a 'home base' of missions from which Chris-

[2] R. K. Orchard, *Missions in a Time of Testing*, London, Lutterworth Press, 1964, p. 39.

tians go 'abroad' to 'unevangelized fields'. All continents need to receive the Gospel anew and to come to terms with its demands and promises. New York and London are as much mission fields as are Calcutta and Tokyo. English villages need a new confrontation with the Gospel no less than do the villages of India and Africa. In principle, of course, this is no new assertion, yet habits of mind are slow to change and much of the institutional expression of the churches' obedience to their mission still perpetuates a distinction between 'home' and 'foreign' missions in a manner which disguises the gravity and depth of the whole world's need for saving news concerning the nature of God and man, the meaning of history and the fulfilment of God's purpose for all humanity. When the Mexico commission directed its attention to the new world of technology, to the significance of the modern city, to the new understanding of the secular and to such urgent contemporary problems as those of poverty or race, it was focusing upon universal issues equally relevant to east and west—that is to 'six continents'. How far does the word 'mission' convey to the average church member and to the average local parish or congregation this largeness of the Christian's task in the world today? How far do the structures of the churches, the missionary societies and committees, the educational and promotional work of missions correspond to this?

Some years prior to the Mexico meeting the World Council's Division of World Mission and Evangelism embarked upon a series of studies and inquiries under the general title of 'The Missionary Structure of the Congregation'. This was an attempt to discover through a number of test cases in various parts of the world to what extent the local church and its organization, equipment, and outlook is manifestly an instrument for furthering the mission of Christ in the world. Some of the results of these investigations have been published in a series called 'World Studies of Churches in Mission'. While each of the studies dealt with a particular situation and in considerable detail, their declared aim was 'to supply insights pertaining to the Church in general and not merely information about the situation investigated'. The areas chosen covered churches in Buganda, Zambia, Togo, Japan, the Congo, the Solomon Islands, and Great Britain. The last named of these studies is of particular interest in that it was conducted by an African sociologist, Dr. K. A. Busia, a deeply committed Christian who is now (1971) Prime Minister of Ghana. When Dr. Busia conducted this inquiry on behalf of the World Council he was a political exile from Ghana and had been spending the years of his exile in academic work in Holland, America, and Great Britain. His chosen area of investigation on behalf of the World Council was in the city of Birmingham, where he concentrated on a group of churches in a mixed urban and suburban area. To these varied local situations he brought a sympathetic mind, a scholarly equipment, and a very searching insight into the strength and weaknesses of the churches. 'The churches are organized', he wrote, 'for those who come inside their doors. The problem is to reach those who are outside. It is for this task that the traditional structures and techniques need to be adapted.' At the close of a volume which contains detailed descriptions and analyses of great interest and importance, Dr. Busia writes:[3]

As I reflect upon the churches of Brookton, their membership so small; spreading themselves over so many fields of activity; winning so few converts; indecisive what to do to instruct and win the young; not giving unequivocal moral leadership to those who look to them for guidance on the burning issues of the day; failing to answer effectively those who, even while they do not reject God, reject the Church and challenge her basic tenets; foot-dragging towards the unity to which they feel impelled; the strongest impression the evidence leaves on my mind is not that the churches are irrelevant but that they lack the boldness that is born of conviction and faith; they seem unable to take drastic steps away from the apparent security of established traditions to meet new situations; yet their proclaimed purpose is to confront all men with a God whose essential character, according to their own message, has been revealed in Christ as love that is also invisible power. Therein lies both judgement and challenge.

'They lack the boldness that is born of conviction and faith.' It is significant that while Dr. Busia's primary area of investigation had to do with the structure of the local congregation, the kind of activities to which the resources of the churches were devoted and the assumptions regarding the obligations of membership in a local church, he could not escape the conclusion that something more was needed than structural change. If the drastic steps to meet new situations were to be perceived and taken something needed to happen in the realm of conviction and faith.

Some years earlier, at the Ghana Assembly of the International Missionary Council, the German theologian and missionary Dr. Walter Freytag spoke of the 'lost directness' of missions. His immediate reference was to the historic missionary societies or mission boards and to vast changes in the whole context of their activity which were making irrelevant many of the traditional policies of

[3] K. A. Busia: *Urban Churches in Britain; a question of relevance* (World Studies of Churches in Mission), London, Lutterworth Press, 1966. The word 'Brookton' in the above quotation is Dr. Busia's fictional equivalent of the name of the part of Birmingham which he was investigating.

missions and the forms in which the missionary imperative had been expressed. Discussing these things with western missionaries living in Asia, Freytag had found 'a widespread feeling of frustration' and amongst leaders of western missionary societies he was given the impression that 'in spite of all their commitment and activity they feel as if they are moving in a fog'.[4] While being greatly concerned with necessary changes in policy and methods within fundamentally new situations, Freytag also saw that the lost directness was part of a deeper uncertainty concerning the ultimate mandate for the Christian mission in an era of theological complexity and confusion. He therefore pointed, with other speakers, to the need for a 'theology of mission' which would be both contemporary in its expression and faithful to the biblical and historical roots of the Christian faith.

This need was a recognized priority in the later years of the International Missionary Council's work and, amongst other attempts to meet it, theologians, missionaries, missionary administrators, and leaders of churches in Asia and Africa participated in a number of consultations and studies on 'The Missionary Obligation of the Church'. Two books in particular were a direct outcome of these studies, one by a Dutch theologian—Johannes Blauw—on *The Missionary Nature of the Church; a survey of the biblical theology of Mission* (1962), and the other by the Asian leader, D. T. Niles, on *The Mission of God and the Missionary Enterprise of the Church* (1962). Both were valuable contributions to a discussion which is still in progress and around which books and articles continue to multiply. If the lost directness is to be recovered and the right new direction discerned, the work of biblical and theological scholars is vital to the task. Yet it is becoming more than ever clear that a full understanding of the Christian mission and the release of new and authentic imperatives for its discharge depends on more than progress in one aspect of theology. It is the faith in its entirety that is under question. It is in relation to life in its wholeness, its complexity and mystery, its terror and splendour that the Christian claims have to be vindicated anew in terms which are meaningful to the mind and convincingly relevant to the needs of the age, the needs of man in society as well as man in his final solitariness on the frontier between life and death. This is a task for the whole Church and for all the churches in every phase of their existence. Therefore in so far as the World Council of Churches can express the churches' united commitment to the task, responsibility has to

[4] Report of the Ghana Assembly of the International Missionary Council, 1958, p. 142.

be carried not by one section of the Council alone but by the whole Council through the integrated activity of all its parts. Succeeding chapters of this book will try to portray both the parts and the whole as they have operated on this frontier of the Church's mission during the last decade.

Inter-Church Aid
To the general public the World Council of Churches is best known through its service to human need. The relief of the homeless, the care and resettlement of refugees, the swift response to the havoc wrought by flood, earthquake, and famine speak a language immediately understood and appreciated even by those who find the blessed word 'ecumenical' uncongenial or incomprehensible. It is significant that during the ten years prior to the formal launching of the World Council at Amsterdam in 1948 the most notable features of the Council's 'process of formation' were its practical service to prisoners of war and displaced persons and its concentration on the impending tasks of post-war reconstruction. Even during wartime, tens of thousands of pounds were raised and expert workers recruited both for immediate relief work and for long-time service. Organizationally these services were operated through a number of agencies, some of them ante-dating by more than a decade the decision to form a World Council of Churches. Notable amongst these was the European Central Bureau for Inter-Church Aid which began its work in 1922 and in 1944 became part of the provisional organization of the World Council. In 1939 this provisional organization established a World Council Secretariat for Non-Aryan Refugees and in 1944 both this secretariat and the European Bureau became part of the provisional committee's Department of Reconstruction and Inter-Church Aid.

Meantime a number of national organizations, working closely with those responsible for shaping the new World Council, entered into the field of relief and reconstruction on a large scale. In the United States, Church World Service was established in 1946, and soon embarked on a great programme of aid towards the resettlement of European refugees and in the help of the devastated churches of Europe, eventually extending its benevolent services to Asia and other parts of the world. In Great Britain the churches joined together to form an organization called Christian Reconstruction in Europe, through which several million pounds were raised for post-war reconstruction. In Germany the year 1945 saw the beginnings of a vast relief organization called Hilfswerker Evangelischen Kirche in Deutschland. All these, and comparable undertakings in other countries, related their work to the policy and

programmes of the emerging World Council of Churches which, on
its inauguration in 1948, included in its structure the organization
which now operates as the Division of Inter-Church Aid, Refugee
and World Service. In the course of all these operations hundreds
of thousands of refugees have been resettled, great relief operations
have been conducted in times of flood, famine, and earthquake,
and in addition to raising vast sums of money for these purposes it
has been possible to provide the personal service of men and women
qualified to deal with the highly technical, legal, and social aspects
of great human problems on an international scale. It is worth
noting that this one division of the World Council, which is financed
independently of the rest of the work of the Council, generally
raises and spends on its service programme in any single year far
more than the cost of the rest of the World Council's operations.

Christian awareness of the most desperate human needs and the
desire to respond to them transcend denominational and confessional boundaries. Even in the years when collaboration in
ecclesiastical concerns between the World Council and the Roman
Catholic Church was seldom achieved and was officially prohibited,
on these frontiers of service to the homeless and the starving there
was close *rapport* and a large amount of common planning between
Roman Catholic relief agencies and the World Council's main service division. When the Second Vatican Council opened the way
for much fuller and officially sponsored joint action, one of the
earliest steps was to convene in Geneva a joint consultation between
the World Council's Division of Inter-Church Aid and the Roman
Catholic Caritas Internationalis. This was followed by further steps
in united action for service and the process is still accelerating.

Large-scale relief operations requiring to be sustained over long
periods inevitably raise questions concerning the relation between
first aid and long-term remedial policies. First aid is a response to
immediate and desperate situations. Long-term remedial action
needs to probe the causes of emergency distress and to be shaped as
far as possible in preventive terms. There are, of course, severe
limits to this. There are disasters humanly unpreventable and suffering which is the consequence of complex national and international
maladies which can only be remedied when the world has found the
way to peace with justice, including economic and racial justice.
Nevertheless within these inescapable limits, the World Council of
Churches has always carried out its first-aid service with keen attention to underlying causes and long-term needs. In ministering, for
example, to the long-drawn-out plight of the refugees in the Middle
East, the work of the Refugee Division has been closely related to
that of the Commission of the Churches on International Affairs.

This body, though ante-dating the First Assembly of the World Council by a year, is an integral part of the Council and is served by a specialist staff which maintains constant liaison with the United Nations and has its representatives in attendance at all meetings of the United Nations Assembly. In such a matter as the deep-seated conflict between the Arab States and Israel this Commission of the World Council has never presumed to act as though it can see solutions when United Nations itself is baffled. It has nevertheless engaged in consultations with both Arabs and Jews and with the responsible agencies in United Nations in the hope of contributing to a right perception of the moral issues at stake and the taking of actions which might lead to better things. In 1951 and 1956 the Commission of the Churches on International Affairs and the Division of Inter-Church Aid, Refugee and World Service jointly convened conferences in Beirut on an international basis for the dual purpose of framing appropriate programmes of relief and of elucidating the long-term issues. These conferences included in their membership not only representatives of the principal churches in the Middle East but experts from outside the churches and officials of United Nations. Another such conference was held in Cyprus in 1969, when the whole situation was reappraised in the light of the 1967 Arab–Israeli war.

Development
In the endeavour to relate its emergency assistance to long-term programmes the Inter-Church Aid Division set up in 1962 a special unit which went by the name of the Committee on Specialized Assistance to Social Projects (SASP). The Division had always been concerned with such matters as improved irrigation and soil conservation in areas liable to famine, and with improved technical education where the lack of it was holding back the progress of a community. These services meant drawing on some of the Division's resources for large and costly projects dependent upon expert planning and execution. SASP, as it was generally known, worked through panels of specialists in agriculture, public health, economic development, education, and various forms of social work, and on the basis of expert planning and costing it recommended to the Division the support of projects likely to make for progress in these areas of need. At the fourth Assembly of the Council at Uppsala in 1968, this unit was reconstructed as the Council's Advisory Committee on Technical Services (ACTS) with responsibility which was defined as 'assessing the technical viability of development projects'.

The term 'development' became another of the most hard-worked words of the fourth Assembly. It initiated a new stage in the process by which first-aid service in response to the most obvious and urgent human needs has compelled the World Council to become more and more involved in questions concerning the right ordering of society. These questions, social and economic with inescapable political implications, have never been absent from the life of the World Council. The main theme of its first Assembly was 'Man's Disorder and God's Design' and two of the four sections of the Assembly's programme were allotted to 'The Church and the Disorder of Society' and 'The Church and the International Disorder'. Under varying titles these themes reappeared at each subsequent assembly and in the on-going work of the Council one of its most active units was the Department on Church and Society. All this was continuous with the task of the earlier Life and Work Movement which became an organic part of the Council on its formation, and which was explicitly focused on the responsibility of the churches 'for making Jesus Christ the Lord not only of the individual heart but of every realm of social, economic and political life'. From 1965 onwards a worldwide series of consultations and investigations was conducted by the Council under the general title of 'The Common Christian Responsibility towards Areas of Rapid Social Change'. The published results of these studies bore such titles as *Africa in transition, Changing Liberia, Christian responsibility in an independent Nigeria, Christian service in the revolution in Indonesia, Christianity in the Asian Revolution* and so on. 'The responsible society', 'responsible revolution' were common themes in all these studies.

By 1966, years of work in this great area of concern culminated in yet another World Conference on Church and Society with its subtitle 'Christians in the technical and social revolutions of our time'. This conference, which did much to determine the tone of the subsequent Fourth Assembly of the Council, was held in Geneva with a membership of over four hundred, the majority of whom were laymen drawn from eighty different countries. Politicians and diplomats, economists, lawyers, doctors, educationists, scientists, engineers and trade unionists, industrialists, financiers, sociologists and journalists outnumbered the churchmen and the theologians, though these were not insignificant either in numbers or competence. About half of the participants came from Asia, Africa, and Latin America. There were eight Roman Catholic observers who were also experts in one or other of the technical subjects on the agenda. Other observers included representatives of the World Jewish Congress, the International Confederation of Free Trade Unions, the International Labour Office, the International Commission of Jurists, the World Health Organization, the Food and Agriculture Organization, the

United Nations Development Programme, the United Nations Educational, Scientific, and Cultural Organization and the Prague Christian Peace Conference—not a bad effort in the collection of representative and acknowledged pundits.

When the World Council's Central Committee in 1962 authorized the setting up of this Geneva conference its resolution declared that 'the time has now come to look at the problems of society in the modern world from the perspective of God's call to man and thus help to develop a body of theological and ethical insights which will assist the churches in their witness in contemporary history'. At a later stage the purposes of the meeting were set out as follows:

> To bring together representatives of the human sciences and those involved in developing new forms of society in the contemporary world as well as theologians:
>
> (1) to examine the following realities in the contemporary world and their implications for human relationships:
>
> the accelerating technological developments of our time
>
> the liberation of peoples from various kinds of dominance together with their new expectation of a fuller life
>
> the growing division between the rich and poor countries
>
> the conflicting interests and consequent power struggle of the nations in an increasingly inter-dependent world;
>
> (2) to recognize the way in which these revolutionary changes have affected and continue to affect Christian discipleship in the modern world;
>
> (3) to consider in the light of such recognition the bearing of the Christian Gospel on thought, on social thought and action:
>
> to formulate for consideration by the churches proposals for the strengthening and renewal of their ministry by society
>
> to help the World Council of Churches in formulating policies which will give expression to a Christian concern for human solidarity, justice, and freedom in a world of revolutionary change.

The preparatory work for the conference included innumerable discussions and meetings of planning groups in various parts of the world. In addition, about three years were spent in the production of four massive volumes of essays or preparatory papers under the following titles:

(1) Christian Social Ethics in a Changing World
(2) Responsible Government in a Revolutionary Age
(3) Economic Growth in a World Perspective
(4) Man in Community

For a fair appraisal of the significance of this whole undertaking these volumes and the official report of the meeting, together with the considerable number of follow-up articles which the conference provoked, need to be studied. In relation to the subsequent work of the World Council of Churches itself, its main emphases and programmes, there were one or two directions in which the Geneva conference was particularly influential.

The first was in the high-lighting of the challenge of the underdeveloped or developing countries to the economically more prosperous areas of the world. The responsibility of the 'haves' towards the 'have nots' began to trouble the conscience of sensitive men a few thousand years before Geneva 1966 and the Christian intensification of this challenge is no new thing. What the Geneva meeting did was to reinforce the contemporary implications of this challenge with a mass of new evidence and with more radical demands, not only upon the individual but upon the whole structure of modern society. Hence the frequency of the word 'revolution' in the Geneva conference and in all that has followed it. One of the basic facts which challenged action is that 70 to 80 per cent of the world's resources are in the hands of about 18 per cent of the world's population and that by the present accepted processes of use and distribution the 'haves' are acquiring more and the 'have nots' possessing less. At present the average *per capita* income in the lands already enjoying a high level of technological and industrial development is about twelve times that which prevails in countries still in an early stage of development. It has been reliably estimated that by the end of this century, unless drastic steps are taken to alter present trends, this disproportion will have become still greater, with the poorer countries 'enjoying' a *per capita* income of about one-eighteenth of that of the highly developed areas of the world.

Disturbing as are these numerical indexes to the situation, the great disparities cannot be measured in income figures alone. They are bound up with resources for personal and community development, with educational and cultural facilities, with economic, political, and social opportunity. The difference is a difference between living and merely existing.

Faced with all that this means in danger to the peace of the world and the well-being of all mankind, the word 'development' has come to stand for one of the great contemporary tasks of Christians, both individually and collectively as the Church. It is for Christians to lead the way in redressing the balance, urging governments to give priority to development projects and pressing economists, social scientists, educationists, and politicians to come to terms with the radical changes needed in the structures of national and international society. Such far-ranging concerns and obligations have, of course, been recognized by far more than the World Council of Churches, its member churches, and service agencies. Many of the notes sounded in the Geneva conference had been sounded a year or two earlier by the Second Vatican Council in its 'Pastoral Constitution on the Church in the Modern World'. 'Some nations,' says the Constitution

with a majority of citizens who are counted as Christians have an abundance of this world's goods while others are deprived of the necessities of life and are tormented with hunger, disease and every kind of misery. This situation must not be allowed to continue to the scandal of humanity. . . . It is now necessary for the family of nations to create for themselves an order which corresponds to modern obligations, particularly with reference to those numerous regions still labouring under intolerable need. . . . The development of any nation depends on human and financial assistance. Through education and professional formation the citizens of each nation should be prepared to shoulder the various offices of economic and social life. Such preparation needs the help of foreign experts. When they render assistance, these experts should do so not in a lordly fashion but as helpers and co-workers. . . .

The developing nations will be unable to procure the necessary material assistance unless the practices of the modern business world undergo a profound change. Additional help should be offered by advanced nations in the form of either grants or investments. These offers should be made generously and without avarice. They should be accepted honourably.

If an economic order is to be created which is genuine and universal there must be an abolition of excessive desire for profit, nationalistic pretentions, the lust for political domination, militarist thinking and intrigues designed to spread and impose ideologies.

While the Vatican Council was in session there were discussions on these common social concerns between those responsible for their handling in Rome and those who were preparing for the Geneva conference. These talks were continued after the Geneva meeting and in 1967 an Exploratory Committee on Society, Development, and Peace began work under the co-chairmanship of Monsignor Joseph Gremillion, Secretary of the Pontifical Commission on Justice and Peace, and a representative of the World Council of Churches, Mr. Max Kohnstamm, a former secretary of the European Iron and Steel Community. This joint body (which subsequently became a permanent standing committee, representing the World Council of Churches and the Vatican and was familiarly known as SODEPAX— the Committee on Society, Development, and Peace) set itself three principal areas for study:

(1) The theological understanding of justice and love in history and society;
(2) A strategy of development in a world perspective;
(3) The development of the full dignity of man in the national, regional, and international community.

This prepared the way for two major conferences in Beirut (1968) and Montreux (1970), both of which were high-powered affairs in their specialist and representative character. They ranged over a great diversity of topics, all bearing upon the better distribution of resources in materials and expertise, technical assistance, government aid, voluntary service, and the role of the churches in pressing for reform through representations to governments, through the education and responsible action of their own members, and through the initiation of at least pilot projects which could act as incentives and, to some extent, point the way forward. An important feature of all these discussions was the manifest desire to go deeper than merely remove the inequalities which had made parts of the world affluent at the expense of others. As the General Secretary of the World Council of Churches, Eugene Carson Blake, expressed it at the Montreux meeting:

The word development as used by the World Council of Churches never means simply a utopian, unrealistic dream of materialistic fulfilment. It refers rather to possible processes whereby the people of the whole world together may establish economic structures of sufficient justice and equality so that men may have a truly human life. We do not suppose that the under-developed nations should simply strive to copy the technological advances of the rich nations. Unless the life and goals of the 'rich' nations are as radically changed in the process of world development as is the life of 'poor' nations, the end of the process will clearly become more like hell on earth than like a heavenly utopia. . . . A community of men using the scientific knowledge and engineering techniques now available but oriented towards a life that is good in a moral and spiritual sense is the concept towards which Christian development programmes must always aim.

Between the Beirut and Montreux meetings the World Council of Churches held its Fourth Assembly at Uppsala where concern for development found expression at fever heat. 'World economic and social development' was the theme allotted to one of the six sections of the Assembly, and various aspects of the subject spilled over into almost all the sections and featured largely in the great plenary sessions of the Assembly, as in the dramatic presentations, the demonstrations and protest songs which enlivened the proceedings. One of the most stirring moments came in a session when President Kenneth Kaunda of Zambia deplored the absence of any sign that the world is becoming 'one world in which dedication to the rights of all human beings without distinction will be a universal phenomenon'. Wars, civil wars, and glaring disparities between rich and poor demonstrate, he said, 'man's refusal to come to terms with reality'. For newly independent nations the 'decade of impatience' has become the 'decade of disillusionment'. 'In a harsh and competitive world,' he added, 'there is desperate need for co-ordinated action between developed and developing countries, but as yet there is not enough political goodwill to achieve this. . . . The developing countries', he continued, 'are not beggars seeking alms; we are participants in the great enterprise of making the world a better and more decent place to live in. What is needed is a new global vision of man and the human race.' It was at this session of the Assembly that the economist, Barbara Ward, taking up a recommendation of the earlier Beirut conference, voiced a passionate challenge to the wealthy nations to adopt a 'world tax' for aid to the less developed countries. 'Is there the will', she asked, 'to adopt a world tax which to begin with might require that wealthy powers give one per cent of their gross material product in genuine economic assistance . . . to put the world's miseries above the upward drift of our ample domestic comforts or, more urgent still, above the world's vast expenditure on a sterile defence . . . to repeal our current slaveries of malnutrition, sickness, ignorance, unemployment, the death of children, the despair of bread-winners, the deserted misery of old age? The only defeat is not to try, so in God's name let us mobilize our resources.'

Following the Uppsala debate the term 'one per cent for development' or 'one per cent for world poverty' became worldwide slogans used in a new crusade by the churches to educate public opinion, enlist press support, rally legislators to the cause and influence governments in order to make the 1970s a decade of development, with the churches backing up their words by the self-assessment of their members to contribute not less than 'one per cent of their take-home pay' to development projects which, valuable in themselves, could also serve both as pilot experiments and incentives to action by government and inter-governmental agencies. Large sums have thus been contributed by the churches over and above their normal giving to missions, Christian Aid, and other undertakings.

Racism

The long process which had its peak moments in the Geneva conference on Church and Society in 1966, with the subsequent world consultations on development at Beirut and Montreux, not only thrust the word development into the thinking of the Uppsala

Assembly. It contributed also to the prominence given in the
Assembly to another provocative term 'racism'. Again, of course,
concern for racial justice and especially for the removal of all dis-
criminations based on colour, had been integral to the life of the
ecumenical movement from the beginning. Christian missions had
for generations been countering racial prejudice by word and deed.
The various movements concerned with Christian social action
which paved the way for the Universal Christian conference on Life
and Work in 1925 were almost invariably involved in the same
issue, and at each Assembly of the World Council from Amsterdam
onwards notable statements on the racial question have been forth-
coming. At the Evanston Assembly in 1954 one of the main sections
was devoted to the subject of 'Inter-Group Relations: the Churches
amid Racial and Ethnic Tensions'. Some influential leaders of the
Dutch Reformed Churches in South Africa were present at this
Assembly and the question of *apartheid* was much to the fore. The
report as 'received by the Assembly and commended to the
churches for study and appropriate action' included the following:

All churches and Christians are involved whether they recognize it or not
in the racial and ethnic tensions of the world but it is in communities
where segregation prevails that they face the plainest difficulties and the
most challenging opportunities; for such segregation denies to those who
are segregated their just and equal rights and results in deep injuries to
the human spirit suffered by offender and victim alike.

The great majority of Christian churches affiliated with the World Council have declared that physical separation within the Church on grounds
of race is a denial of spiritual unity and of the brotherhood of man. Yet
such separations persist within these very churches and we often seek to
justify them on other grounds than race because in our own hearts we
know that separation solely on the grounds of race is abhorrent in the eyes
of God.

We seek to justify such exclusion on the ground of difference of culture
or on the ground that a residential pattern of segregation necessitates it or
on the ground that the time is not yet ripe. We even say that we are willing
to abandon all separations but must retain them because so many others
are unwilling to abandon them. We often make use of the unregenerate-
ness of the world to excuse our own. The Church is called upon, therefore, to set aside such excuses and to declare God's will both in words
and deeds.

The Church of Christ cannot approve of any law which discriminates on
grounds of race, which restricts the opportunity of any person to acquire
education, to prepare himself for his vocation, to procure or to practise
employment in his vocation, or in any other way curtails his exercise of
the full rights and responsibilities of citizenship and of sharing in the
responsibilities and duties of government.

Following the reception of the statement from which these extracts are taken the Assembly adopted a formal resolution declaring 'its conviction that any form of segregation based on race, colour or ethnic origin is contrary to the Gospel and is incompatible with the Christian doctrine of man and with the nature of the Church of Christ. The Assembly urges the churches within its membership to renounce all forms of segregation or discrimination and to work for their abolition within their own life and within society.' Three delegates from the Dutch Reformed Churches abstained from voting on this resolution and in a dignified and courteous statement said:

We do not intend to record our votes against what is being proposed. At this stage we dare not commit our churches either way, but wish to keep the door open for further conversation. . . . We appreciate the argument that no resolution of this Assembly has mandatory power over member churches and that certain recommendations, especially this resolution, are intended to stimulate the independent thought and action of certain churches in specific situations, but we feel constrained to say that at this stage of our ecumenical discussions on these matters it may have the opposite effect by so prejudicing the issues at stake for some churches that fruitful action for them will be gravely jeopardized. . . . We wish to place on record that we have experienced at Evanston much evidence of what we truly believe to be real Christian good will and an attempt to understand the peculiar difficulties we have to face. In response to that we now pledge ourselves personally to the task of urging our respective churches to apply themselves as urgently as possible to the study of the report and to communicate their findings to the Central Committee as soon as possible.

Following the Evanston Assembly an important conference on the racial question was held in South Africa. It was attended by representatives of the eight member churches of the World Council in South Africa and by a delegation from the World Council of Churches led by the Chairman of its Central Committee. The consultation marked some real advance in agreement and especially in mutual understanding and respect. Nevertheless it was followed by the withdrawal from membership of the World Council of those synods of the Dutch Reformed Churches which had been amongst its foundation members.

It will be seen that the racial question did not wait for the Uppsala Assembly to deal with it in fundamental fashion. Nevertheless the issue flared up at Uppsala in a manner which constituted a vivid and tumultuous new stage in the long debate. Again, the Geneva Conference of 1966 had spoken vigorously about the worsening situation throughout the world and it had related the increase in racial tensions to the great and widening economic disparities between developed and developing countries. 'The tensions', said the report, 'between the affluent segments of society which happen to be predominantly white and the disinherited segments which happen to be predominantly non-white are more acute than ever before.' This 'explosive situation' must now be reckoned with as 'an acute power-struggle. . . . Disinherited racial groups are desperately struggling to achieve social justice by organizing themselves to gain political and economic power as in African nationalisms and in Black Power in the USA.' While reaffirming earlier statements of the World Council on race, the Conference put increasing emphasis on Christian *political* responsibility in the pursuit of racial justice. It urged 'Christians and churches everywhere'

(1) to oppose openly and actively the perpetuation of the myth of racial superiority as it finds expression in social conditions and human behaviour as well as in laws and social structures;

(2) to engage in the common task of changing the structure of society through legislation, social planning and corporate action and to mobilize all its resources to ensure the full and equal participation of all racial and ethnic groups in the corporate life of a pluralistic society;

(3) to recognize, support and share the individual and collective interests of people who are disadvantaged by their race and ethnic origin, so that they may gain the basic human, political and economic rights enjoyed by the others in a pluralistic society.

At Uppsala such pleas as these became more vehement and the temper of the Assembly, especially that of the large and vociferous youth group, was one which responded readily to the bitter invective of James Baldwin, the novelist, who introduced himself as 'one of God's creatures whom the Christian Church has most betrayed', and who had 'always been outside the Church, even when I tried to work in it'. 'I wonder', he declared, 'if there is left in the Christian civilizations the moral energy, the spiritual daring, to atone, to repent and to be born again.'

In view of the time and energy which members of the Assembly, individually and collectively, gave to the subject it was surprising that a document on racism intended for the Assembly's reception proved to be so poor in form and substance that it was withdrawn. Instead of making a statement of its own the Assembly therefore passed the responsibility to the Central Committee. A year later, at its meeting in Canterbury in 1969, the matter came before the Central Committee which also had presented to it the report of an 'International Consultation on Racism' which had been held at Notting Hill, London, the scene of some fairly recent ugly racial conflicts. This consultation had been convened by the World Council's staff and it made headline news when its proceedings were violently interrupted by some Black Power leaders. Out of the tumult there emerged a proposal for 'an ecumenical programme to combat racism' which was later adopted in revised form by the Central Committee. The document outlining the proposed programme recognized that 'the World Council has offered a strong lead in the past but its studies and statements generally have evoked neither adequate awareness nor effective action'. The document acknowledged that 'white racism is not the only form' which the evil takes. In some parts of the world, for example 'like Asia and Africa other forms of racism and ethno-centricism provide the most crucial problems'. Nevertheless the statement argued that the 'accumulation of wealth and power in the hands of white peoples' 'necessitated a special focus on white racism'. In its summons to the churches this programme to combat racism included the following:

(1) We call upon the churches to move beyond charity, grants and traditional programming to relevant and sacrificial action leading to new relationships of dignity and justice among all men, and to become agents for the radical reconstruction of society. There can be no justice in our world without a transfer of economic resources to undergird the redistribution of political power and to make cultural self-determination meaningful. In this transfer of resources a corporate act by the ecumenical fellowship of churches can provide a significant moral lead.
(2) We call upon churches to confess their involvement in the perpetuation of racism. Churches should make an analysis of their financial situation in order to determine the degree to which their financial practices, domestic and international, contribute to the support of radically oppressive governments, discriminatory industries and inhuman working conditions. The impact will be greater if this is an ecumenical act.
(3) The forces seeking to liberate non-white peoples from the oppressive yoke of white racism have appropriately demanded the participation of religious institutions in restoring wealth and power to people. We urge churches to make land available freely or at low cost to radically oppressed groups for community and economic development. Churches which have benefited from radically exploitative economic systems should immediately allocate a significant portion of their total resources without employing paternalistic mechanisms of control to organizations of the racially oppressed or organizations supporting the victims of racial injustice.

In the conviction that the situation now called for more than another set of resolutions reaffirming previous statements, the Central Committee at Canterbury agreed to make special administrative provision for pursuing the programme to combat racism. It authorized the appointment, under the direction of the General Secretary, of three new staff members (an Executive Secretary, an Officer for Ecumenical and International Relations and a Secretary for Research and Documentation) with necessary clerical staff and funds for travel, research, and publications, at an estimated cost of $150,000 a year for five years. This was to be met from three sources, namely the General Budget of the Council, the Service Programme of the Division of Inter-Church Aid, Refugee and World Service and the funds of the Division of World Mission and Evangelism. In addition, the Committee authorized the creation of a special Capital Fund to which $200,000 of the Council's reserves would be transferred and to which the churches would be asked to contribute at least $300,000. The fund was designated 'for distribution to organizations of oppressed racial groups or organizations supporting victims of racial injustice whose purposes are not inconsonant with the general purposes of the World Council . . . to be used in their struggle for economic, social and political justice'. The Executive Committee was given authority to decide, in the light of recommendations from a specially appointed International Advisory Committee which organizations would be assisted from this fund.

Something of a furore was created when publicity was given in 1970 to a first list of beneficiaries. These included a number of 'liberation' movements in Angola, Mozambique, Guinea-Bissau, Rhodesia and South Africa some of which were politically banned and were explicitly directed to the overthrow of white ruling minorities. Certain of them were avowedly involved in guerrilla activities. Since the over-ruling condition attached to the grants was that they should be used for purposes 'not inconsonant with the general purposes of the World Council' it was assumed by the Executive Committee that this would exclude their application to violent action. In fact most of the grants were expressly related to educational and social welfare purposes, to the provision of legal aid for political prisoners and the relief of the families of detainees and freedom fighters. At the Central Committee in Addis Ababa in 1971 satisfaction was expressed that assurances had been given by all these organizations that the grants would not be used for military purposes. Nevertheless controversy continued for some time regarding the appropriateness of this action. Much of the trouble arose from press and public interpretations of it as 'World Council help to guerrilla fighters', but apart from such a misinterpretation there were those who questioned the possibility of effectively separating the humanitarian needs of the organizations in question from their total policy. There were others who felt that the existing procedures for authorizing action in such controversial matters needed to be revised in order to ensure fuller consultation with member churches and national councils and to secure the churches' more explicit concurrence.

Beyond such aspects of the matter as these, two clear issues at least have emerged on which there can be little difference of opinion between the member churches of the World Council. The first is that the racial question stands out as one of the most critical issues for the modern world, and that Christian responsibility demands commitment and involvement. Verbal resolutions are not enough. Both word and act must must also make it clear that the Christian Church stands with the oppressed and against the oppressors. Secondly, there is the urgent need for fresh consideration by Christians and between the churches of the validity or non-validity of violent means in the pursuit of just ends. When injustice is perpetrated by tyrannical governments enforcing their policies by the most inhuman and destructive instruments of power can any form of violent resistance be given a Christian sanction? No doubt in the more rigorous pursuit of the right answer to this question deep disagreements of the kind which already exist will further appear, but the necessity to face the agonizing problem from an ecumenical standpoint and with a realistic appraisal of the world situation today can scarcely be questioned. It was for this reason that at its meeting at Addis Ababa in 1971 the World Council's Central Committee returned to a resolution of the Uppsala Assembly of 1968. This was a resolution passed as a memorial to Martin Luther King in the course of which the Central Committee was asked 'to explore means by which the World Council could promote studies on non-violent methods of achieving social change'. A brief discussion on ways and means of implementing this proposal took place at Canterbury in 1969 and at Addis Ababa it was decided to ask the churches for funds to make possible a two-year process of study and consultation under the direction of a member of the staff of the Department on Church and Society.

Means and Ends

'Service and the Responsible Society.' Even the most instinctive acts of service to those in desperate need raise questions about ends as well as means. Emergency necessities become the symptoms of long-term needs. These again provoke questioning about the structures and practices of a society within which such needs become crying needs. These questions still further compel deeper analyses not only of the springs of human behaviour but of the meaning of life itself. They call for a fresh understanding of the ends and means which God has disclosed in the person of the Word made flesh, that Word which is always personal and in whom all things cohere. Churches which care about acting together on the basis of a common faith are insistently driven to explore the relation between action and belief. Thus the service agencies of the World Council of Churches can only achieve their ends in the right integrated relationship with the whole of the Council's witness. As one of the reports received by the Central Committee at Addis Ababa in 1971 said:

Decisions in the realm of secular action must be strengthened not only through formal worship gatherings but through more faithful devotion to the unshaken centre and source of our Christian daily life, namely, our faith in Christ and our experience of our common calling to act together in the world. The emphasis on social action must be supported by a deeper existential sharing in the spiritual inheritance of the Gospel and the *kerygma* of the *ecclesia*. No kind of church action can be separated from faith and it should not weaken our conviction and total commitment through the Church to the one Lord of the whole world. On the contrary, it is this which is decisive as both the source and the criterion of all social activity.

Christian Unity
Within the administrative and committee structure of the World
Council of Churches there is no unit solely concerned with
theology, no such body as a standing commission of theologians.
Theological questions underlie all the work of the Council, of
course, and they become explicit in relation to some of its important
tasks. Responsibility for dealing with them, however, is distributed
throughout the organization rather than concentrated in a single
specialist group. From time to time and in relation to a particular
issue the Council solicits the services of theologians from all the
churches and confessions. In the formative years of the movement
such scholars as Karl Barth, Emil Brunner, Reinhold Niebuhr, Ingve
Brilioth, Leonard Hodgson, Andrej Nygren, John Baillie, John
Mackay, and C. H. Dodd were closely involved in the Council's
work, especially in the preparatory studies leading up to the main
themes of assemblies. The succession has continued and at some
point or other almost every department of the Council's work re-
lies on the willingness of theologians of all nationalities to give
counsel and serve on committees or working parties concerned with
the theological presuppositions of particular tasks.

It is in the area of faith and order that the most constant and
systematic help of theologians has been called for. Structurally the
work of the historic Faith and Order Movement centres on the
Commission on Faith and Order which consists of not more than
150 members and which normally meets every three years. The
Commission is served by a Secretariat, whose principal member is
styled 'Director', and by a small Working Committee meeting
annually. On the initiative of the Commission, world conferences
on Faith and Order are convened from time to time. These conferences have proved to constitute some of the most significant land-
marks in the history of the ecumenical movement. Four have been
held—two before the formation of the World Council (Lausanne
1927 and Edinburgh 1937), and two under the auspices of the
Council (Lund 1952 and Montreal 1963).

As defined in the Council's Constitution, the primary function of
the Faith and Order Commission is 'to proclaim the oneness of the
Church of Jesus Christ and to keep prominently before the Council
and also before churches within and outside its membership the

obligation to manifest that unity for the sake of their Lord and for the better accomplishment of his mission in the world'. The Constitution lays down what it describes as 'cardinal principles' which must be observed in all the activities of the Commission. These are:

(1) That its main work is to draw churches into conversation and study in such a way that none is asked to be disloyal to its convictions or to compromise them, and all are invited to share reciprocally in giving and receiving. In the conduct of such conversations differences are to be recorded as honestly as agreements.
(2) That only the churches themselves are competent to initiate steps towards union by entering into negotiations with one another. The work of the Commission is to act on their invitation as helper and adviser.

Just before his death in 1970, Dr. Marc Boegner's reminiscent volume, *L'Exigence Oecuménique*, was published in an English translation under the title *The Long Road to Unity*. Dr. Boegner was one of those ecumenical pioneers who saw in the World Conference on Faith and Order at Lausanne in 1927 a new ray of light on the path ahead, that path which would resolve at long last the great historic divisions between the churches. The road still proves to be a long one and its direction is not always luminous. But even those who have been most realistic about the difficulties and disappointed by the slowness have nevertheless persisted in the search for those ways of expressing our given unity in Christ which are in keeping with his will and purpose. They continue to do so believing that upon the realization of this unity depends our understanding of the full meaning and power of the Gospel and its convincing communication to the world.

As the Constitution indicates, the World Council does not itself initiate schemes of union nor take responsibility for their negotiation. This is solely the business of the churches themselves. However, it is scarcely possible to dissociate the many schemes of union achieved or embarked upon during the last few decades from the influence of the Faith and Order movement. No serious thinking about the Church and its future could ignore all that the movement has signified in its challenge to the disunity of the churches, its fundamental study of the causes of disunity, historical, theological and non-theological, and the ecumenical discussion which it has promoted on the nature of the Church, the ministry and the Sacraments, or the relation of mission to unity. Most of the leaders in the negotiation of schemes of union in various parts of the world have at some time or other been involved in a Faith and Order meeting. They have found themselves helped in their particular local endeavours by the movement's formulation and elucidation of problems which are universal. This interplay has been assisted by the growth of regional conferences on Faith and Order, convened by local councils of churches, not by the World Council itself. These have concentrated on unity issues from the standpoint of a particular country or region. Notable meetings of this kind have been held in New Zealand (1955), India, Indonesia, the Philippines, Japan, and the U.S.A. (1957), England (1964), and Hong Kong (1966, under the auspices of the East Asia Christian Conference. The strength of these regional conferences has lain in their local initiation, but contact has naturally been maintained with the Faith and Order Commission whose experience and resources have contributed greatly to the result. While constantly emphasizing the advisory character of the Commission's role it has been made clear that its services are readily available in relation to any projected union negotiations. Speaking of this role at the meeting of the Commission in 1967 the Chairman—Bishop Oliver Tomkins—regarded it as something more than proffering advice on technicalities. 'We have a function,' he said, 'to help the churches to find true discrimination, the ability to learn from God when and how to decide.'[1]

In 1967, at the request of a number of churches involved in union discussions, the secretariat of the Faith and Order Commission convened a Consultation on Church Union Negotiations in Geneva. This was designed as an opportunity to exchange information on the nature of the various schemes under discussion so that experience in one area could be related to negotiations in another. The participants in this Consultation came from twenty-six different countries and were involved in twenty-seven actual schemes of union. Like all such gatherings, the consultation carried no executive authority but in the light of this sharing of information and experience a number of recommendations were made to the churches. These included the proposal that while negotiations in any given instance were proceeding the participating churches should 'covenant together' on terms which would make inter-communion possible prior to the achievement of actual union. Three years later another of these consultations was held at Limuru in Kenya. Amongst the emphases apparent throughout these 1970 discussions much was said about the importance of regarding any achieved act of union in a particular place as simply an interim step towards the achievement of a more comprehensive union. 'United churches exist with a view to the whole ecumenical movement,' said the report of this consultation:

[1] *New Directions in Faith and Order* (Faith and Order Paper No. 50), Geneva, 1928, p. 165.

They do not come into being to defend and protect a newly acquired identity. They exist for preparing wider union. It would therefore be more correct not to speak of united churches but rather to use the term uniting churches. United churches must therefore be prepared for the encounter with other churches, even with churches which represent entirely different traditions.

In contemplating larger and more comprehensive unions the Limuru meeting recognized the need for diversity in the patterns of the unity being sought:

Organic or corporate union does not refer to only one pattern of union. The following are conditions which must be fulfilled to achieve organic union: A common basis of faith; a common name; full commitment to one another, including the readiness to give up separate identity; the possibility of taking decisions together and of carrying out the missionary task as circumstances require. These conditions leave room, however, for various models of union which may be adopted according to cultural or other needs.

It will be seen that the Faith and Order movement has through the years become much more than an activity of the World Council. It is far more than a series of world conferences held at lengthy intervals, or a succession of studies initiated by the Council. It is a movement amongst the churches, amongst groups of churches. It operates within national councils and regional councils. It engages the prolonged study of theologians and church administrators and finds expression in innumerable consultations, formal and informal. Through its own Commission and Secretariat on Faith and Order the World Council tries to keep aware of all this, to appraise its significance, to see the parts in relation to the whole, to take initiatives and be of service wherever there is a readiness to accept such service.

One important feature of the Commission's life from the beginning (and this was characteristic of the Faith and Order movement before it became embodied in the World Council) has been its ability to secure the co-operation of representatives of churches not in membership with the World Council, whether the Roman Catholic Church or churches which stand apart from the Council on grounds commonly described as Conservative Evangelical. This has made possible valuable discussions, for example, with Seventh Day Adventists. This openness of the Commission facilitated an important step which was taken at the Uppsala Assembly when the Roman Catholic Church accepted a proposal that it should appoint official representatives to the membership of the Faith and Order Commission even though the question of Roman Catholic membership in the Council itself was still a distant one.

Inter-Confessional Dialogue

Another recent extension of the Commission's work and relationships has been in connexion with the 'World Families of Churches', or 'World Confessional Organizations', to which reference has been made in a previous chapter. Even those who hope that these organizations will eventually prove to be transitory recognize that they represent great and distinctive traditions which need to be reckoned with in their theological significance if the churches are to reach a full understanding and realization of their unity and mission. The Faith and Order Commission has therefore sought ways and means of engaging these organizations, both in its own studies and consultations and in 'inter-confessional dialogue' with one another. In 1967 the organizations were asked to appoint liaison representatives to the Faith and Order Commission as research consultants in addition to sending fraternal delegates to meetings of the Commission. Further the Faith and Order Secretariat has been closely associated with these world families in some extremely important inter-confessional discussions. The most fruitful of these has been between the Lutheran World Federation and the World Alliance of Reformed Churches—two international groups which represent two major traditions stemming from the Reformation, the Lutheran and the Calvinistic.[2] Since 1962 there has been a parallel series of meetings in Europe and the United States in which leading theologians and churchmen from both confessions have been examining afresh the historic differences between them, and the relation of these two great traditions to contemporary thought on the nature of the Gospel and the Church.

In 1970 a Joint Committee of the Lutheran World Federation and the World Alliance of Reformed Churches surveyed the progress of these discussions and endorsed the conclusion reached in both the American and European consultations that earlier 'doctrinal condemnations' of Reformed churches by Lutherans and Lutheran churches by Reformed as embodied in the historic confessions of both bodies 'had been rendered obsolete by theological

---

[2] While the member churches of the World Alliance of Reformed Churches have in the past mainly reflected the Calvinism of Reformed or Presbyterian churches, the Alliance has always included some churches whose history and ethos bear the marks of other Reformation influences, e.g. that of Zwingli and of more radical reformers such as the Anabaptists. This diversity of elements in the membership of the Reformed Alliance was increased in 1970 when the former International Congregational Council joined with the Alliance in forming the new World Alliance of Reformed Churches (Presbyterian and Congregational). While Calvinistic influences are far from negligible in historic Congregationalism there is a marked affinity between Congregationalism and the faith and practice of the more radical reformers.

developments and the remaining differences in ecclesiastical doctrine, order, and style of life possess no church-separating significance'.[3] The European meetings, which were originally sponsored by the Faith and Order Department, further proposed that a 'concordat' should be established between the two confessions which would make possible 'full pulpit and altar fellowship'. This proposal is being pursued and there is every sign that something along this line will be achieved. It is worth noting that while the representatives of both the Lutheran World Federation and the World Alliance of Reformed Churches welcomed the greater cohesion that this would give to two groups of churches stemming from the Reformation, they declared that they 'do not envisage the establishment of their fellowship as the building of a bloc of churches of the Reformation. They see it rather within the horizon of the coming together of all churches.'[3]

In the published report of the American discussions between Lutheran and Reformed churchmen[4] there is the interesting admission that 'at some points we have discovered that our respective views of each other have been inherited caricatures initially caused by misunderstanding or polemical zeal'. This admission is of wider application: it goes indeed to the heart of many situations in which for far too long churches and Christian people have remained insulated from one another in disunities which have lost whatever original justification they may have possessed. This is not the whole story, of course, particularly in relation to the great divide between Catholic and Protestant in the Reformation and subsequently. Yet even here the long persistence of inherited caricatures has played, and still plays, its divisive role.

At this point another feature of the Faith and Order movement— recognizing this to be more than an activity of the World Council— has in recent years proved to be fruitful, especially in the removal of misunderstandings and the correction of distorted images. There is in process a series of what are generally referred to as bilateral conversations or dialogues between the Roman Catholic Church and the other principal confessions. While these have been initiated by, and remain the responsibility of the confessions, the Faith and Order Secretariat of the World Council has been kept in touch with them and in some instances has participated in them. Involved in these discussions are the Lutheran World Federation, the World

---

[3] From the *Report of the Lutheran and Reformed Consultations in Leuenberg*, Switzerland, 1969–70, see *Reformed and Presbyterian World*, June 1969, Vol. XXX No. 6.

[4] *Marburg Revisited*, edited by Paul C. Empey and James I. McCord, Minneapolis, Augsburg Publishing House, 1966.

Alliance of Reformed Churches, the World Methodist Council, the Anglican Communion and the Old Catholics. The subjects under discussion include the Gospel and the Church, Revelation and History, the Relationship of Christ to the World, Justification and Sanctification, Scripture and Tradition, the Authority of the Church, the Ministry and the Sacraments.

Relationships between the Roman Catholic Church and the Orthodox Churches have always been of a special character because of the radical separation and the common traditions of these two great confessions. Here again, significant discussions have been in process for some years. These have been part of that changing relationship which made it possible for Pope Paul VI and the Ecumenical Patriarch Athenagoras I to meet in the Holy Land in 1964 and to exchange visits in 1967 and 1968 between Rome and Istanbul. Most significantly, in 1965, just before the close of the Second Vatican Council, the mutual excommunications which had been in operation for eight hundred years between the Orthodox and Roman Catholic Churches were formally lifted. Another series of contacts, following an initiative of the Faith and Order Department, has been developed between the Orthodox Churches and the Ancient Oriental Churches. Since 1964 a number of consultations have taken place between representatives of these two traditions, with encouraging results in the growth of theological accord between the Chalcedonian and non-Chalcedonian Churches.

All this represents more than an easing of diplomatic relationships between ecclesiastics and their institutions. Fundamentally it is part of that theological development of which the ecumenical movement itself is an expression, and which derives from a fresh approach to the content of the Faith and the meaning of Order and which of necessity goes on to consider the relation of the past to the present, of the unchanging to the changing, of the nature of the universal Church and its contemporary calling and obedience. The pursuit of these questions in their full theological significance, as well as in their practical implications, is an exercise in which churches have been led to engage together in a mutual trust which removes the fear of proselytizing and the dangers of compromising. What the end will be cannot be foreseen but the beginning and the continuing in the process has become, for the deepest reasons, an obligation on all who profess and call themselves Christians.

Tradition and Traditions
In the specific tasks of the World Council's Faith and Order Commission and the work of its Secretariat some recent trends need to be seen in the light of the whole process which began organizationally

with the first World Conference on Faith and Order at Lausanne
in 1927. The period between Lausanne and the third World
Conference at Lund in 1952 was largely concerned with elucidating
the differences between the churches and expounding, analysing,
and comparing the traditions out of which these differences had
emerged. This was a kind of comparative examination of the
doctrines, the principles of order and the liturgical practices of the
different confessions or denominations. It made clearer the different conceptions of the Church, the Ministry, and the Sacraments
which had arisen in Christian history. It revealed and elaborated
different understandings of the meaning of Catholicity and of the
idea of unity. To some extent this was a defensive process in which
each of the churches was eager to expound to the others the real
character of its own tradition and witness. Yet it was not merely
defensive. All who were involved in the process confessed their profound dissatisfaction with the disunity of the churches and their
desire to perceive and achieve the unity which Christ wills. Further,
the process of elucidation contributed greatly towards growth in
understanding and in mutual respect. Some of the most important
consequences of these years were personal—the creation and nurture
of friendships rooted in a common confession of Christ and in a
common search for his will. This in itself became a constantly renewed incentive to press on with the search. It constituted for many
a new experience of the unity already given in Christ.

By the time the Lund meeting occurred, however, there was a
widespread feeling that this exercise in comparisons had run its
course. To spend more time in elucidating history and defining the
existing situation seemed unlikely to produce fresh light on the way
ahead. As one of the veterans of the movement said at Lund, 'Can
we go on for ever and ever round and round in the same circle
explaining ourselves to one another?'[5] The long comparative approach had led to a *cul de sac*. Not inappropriately a journalistic
appraisal of the situation was entitled 'The Ecumenical Dead End
Kids'. Recognizing the need for a fresh start, the Lund meeting
shifted the direction of the Faith and Order studies and consultations. The new road was marked by three main features. First, the
great and basic questions concerning the nature of the Church and
its ministry, the significance of worship, and the meaning of unity
were now to be approached not from any of the existing positions
but by a united endeavour to penetrate behind the historical differences to the origins of the Faith and of the Church as these are to
be seen in the Person and Work of Christ. As the Lund report put
it, the aim was 'to penetrate behind the divisions of the Church on

[5] *See Evanston to New Delhi*, Geneva, W.C.C., 1961, p. 37.

earth to our common faith in the one Lord'. Commenting on this
new endeavour, Bishop Nygren said:

We would not dare to think that the differences developed in the course
of centuries between the churches could be removed simply by our
theological discussions, but what we can do is to trace the questions
down to their roots and back to Christ. If the Church, its nature and its
working, are looked upon in the light of Christ then also these questions
are seen in a new light. The problems among us do not disappear but
they are understood on both sides in a different way. . . . If the churches
learn to understand one another from the centre, from Christ, then also
the problems between the churches will gradually find solution.[6]

This new approach to the problems of Faith and Order—often referred to as the 'Christological method'—proved fruitful at the
crucial point of disclosing how much positive agreement there was
amongst the churches on the fundamentals of the faith. The differences in the formulation of the faith and the ordering of the
churches' life remain, but in any further attempt to deal with the
differences there was the growing realization that these rested on
deeply shared convictions—what the Lund report described as
'that common history which we have as Christians and which we
have discovered to be longer, larger and richer than any of our
separate histories in our divided churches'. A signal outcome of this
approach is to be seen in the progress achieved over the years on the
theme of 'Tradition and traditions'. Amidst the diversity of forms
which the traditions of the churches have taken there is to be
discovered the Tradition which (as the Montreal Faith and Order
Conference defined it) is 'the Gospel itself, transmitted from generation to generation in and by the Church, Christ himself present in
the life of the Church'. What the several traditions seek to trans-
mit is 'the Christian faith, not only as a sum of tenets but as a
living reality transmitted through the operation of the Holy Spirit'.
From the common ground provided by this discrimination it has
been found possible to reach new elucidations and agreements
across what have hitherto been assumed to be conflicting traditions.

The other two features of this new period involved a departure
from the strictly theological studies—or rather, these were now
supplemented by another range of inquiry and analysis. It was here
that the phrase 'non-theological factors' commanded increasing
attention. It was not only on questions of doctrine that the Church
in the course of its history had divided and sub-divided. Social and
cultural factors, politics and race had all played their part. There
were psychological reasons for the estrangement of persons from one
another within the Christian fellowship and for the disintegration

[6] *Evanston to New Delhi*, pp. 38–39.

of the fellowship itself. These factors were none the less potent; indeed they could be more intractable because it was possible for them to be hidden by ostensible doctrinal differences. They might even be given a theological colouring and elevated into differences of principle or doctrine. In addressing itself to these non-theological factors, the Faith and Order movement was endeavouring to probe further into the real situation presented by the disunity of the churches. The term 'unmasking' was sometimes used to describe the process. Not fundamental and insoluble doctrinal differences but attitudes, loyalties, and tenacities induced by sociological or psychological factors could account for some ecclesiastical separations.

One phase of this particular direction in Faith and Order can be seen in a series of studies on 'institutionalism'. These were basically sociological examinations of the structure of certain denominations, the sources which had shaped them and which rendered them either resistant to change or responsive to new situations. As the study asserted, its purpose was 'not to deny the positive and constructive value of institutional forms but to help the churches to become aware of perversions of patterns of life which in themselves may have the right and proper function'. It sought to indicate 'those points at which commitment to forms of organization and other factors of a highly relative character create strains between the churches and stand in the way of unity'. Just as the new movement in the doctrinal studies sought to press behind the historic traditions to the beginning of the Christian tradition, so the sociological studies endeavoured to analyse the forms of historic institutions in order to distinguish between their changing and permanent features. In the nature of such inquiries and studies, precise results can scarcely be tabulated. What can be said with confidence is that these two processes have on the one hand contributed to a more rigorous self-criticism within both institutions and traditions. On the other hand they have brought churchmen closer to one another in a common desire to rediscover the abiding elements in the faith and form of the Church and the criteria by which all diversities and changes are to be tested.

The third of these new directions which characterize the period following the Lund Faith and Order Conference—and the second of the non-theological processes—is illustrated in the so-called 'Lund principle' which was enunciated in the message of the Conference. The heart of this lay in the plea that churches should 'act together in all matters except those in which deep differences of conviction compel them to act separately'. 'The measure of unity which it has been given to the churches to experience together', said the Lund message, 'must now find clearer manifestation.'

A faith in the one Church of Christ which is not implemented by *acts* of obedience is dead. There are truths about the nature of God and his Church which will remain for ever closed to us unless we act together in obedience to a unity which is already ours. We would therefore earnestly request our churches to consider whether they are doing all they ought to do to manifest the oneness of the people of God. Should not our churches ask themselves whether they are showing sufficient eagerness to enter into conversations with other churches and whether they should not act together in all matters except those in which deep differences of conviction compel them to act separately?[7]

It is important to recognize that this call for unity-in-action did not imply any abandonment of the search for unity-in-order and structure. It was not substituting co-operation for unity, nor did the argument rest only on the practical advantages of doing things together. There was the conviction that in the process of doing things together new insights would be given and new power released which would further the great end of unity. Again it would be impossible to list the number of instances in which the Lund principle has been acted upon or to appraise the consequences of such action in opening the way to further progress. The actual wording of this historic plea can still—twenty years after—be seen and heard in fresh contemporary challenges and ventures, in relation to innumerable aspects of the churches' life and work. Although far more might have been accomplished if the response had been greater, there can be little doubt that much of the progress achieved during these two decades in local co-operation generally and in growing confidence between the churches has at least been greatly aided by acting on the Lund principle. The fruits of this can be seen in fresh experiments in the more ecumenical training of the ministry, in the provision of industrial and university chaplaincies, as well as in such practical projects as Christian Aid. It can also be safely assumed that some of the achieved schemes of union and others still under discussion have been aided by the experience of Christians in learning to 'act together in all matters except those in which deep differences of conviction compel them to act separately'.

The Wholeness of the Church and of the World

Despite the new start after Lund and the steady increase in the number of churches involved in union negotiations, the Faith and Order movement has continued to be disturbed by a sense of dissatisfaction with its own achievements and the slow progress amongst the churches towards the ultimate goal. The impatience which found expression in 1952 over the round-and-round exercise

[7] Quoted in *The Ecumenical Movement*, by Norman Goodall, London, O.U.P., 2nd ed., 1964, pp. 214–15.

in mutual explanation was renewed a dozen years later when the secretary of the Faith and Order Commission, Dr. Lukas Vischer, said 'We cannot go on for decades talking of meeting, dialogue, conversation and better understanding. Unless definite results follow joy in the ecumenical movement must turn to disappointment.' Dr. Lukas Vischer was here addressing a meeting of the Faith and Order Commission at Aarhus, Denmark, in 1964. 'In many respects', he added 'isolation has been broken through. We know one another; indeed we know one another only too well. When we meet for ecumenical conferences the first impression is not the discovery of new faces but the comforting feeling of being together again among old friends. We have already discussed the differences which separate us so often that there is really no point in repeating the exercise, at least not unless it can be done in a completely new way.' Despite this feeling of impatience the movement had, in fact, continued to move during the preceding decade, and had been trying out new ways in the exercise of getting beyond differences to agreements. Years of study and consultation based on the 'Christological method' had not only led to a widespread realization of the fundamental unity in Christ; it had opened up fresh areas for elucidation and these were being pursued at a new depth of common commitment to a great end. For example, granted a common acceptance of the Lordship of Christ over the Church and the world, in what ways is this Lordship exercised in relation to nature, to history and to contemporary events? Again, how is the presence of Christ realized and discerned in the Church? What is the special significance of the Sacraments in relation to this? Or again, if the Holy Spirit testifies to something more than once-upon-a-time divine actions, how are the Spirit's contemporary operations to be discerned? If worship represents a moment and an experience in which Christ's Lordship is acknowledged, and his living presence in the Spirit is apprehended, what are the essential and unchanging elements in worship and what changing forms will best testify to the unchanging yet ever-renewed reality? Innumerable discussions and studies on such questions as these were initiated and fostered by the Faith and Order movement during the period up to the Uppsala Assembly of the Council in 1968. In all of these studies fundamental agreements became far more evident than radical disagreements. This was particularly true—for some it proved to be surprisingly true—in relation to a joint study on the Eucharist where an impressive consensus was reached on the essential meaning of this 'gift of God to his Church'.[8]

[8] See *Report of the Fourth World Conference on Faith and Order* (Montreal, 1963), Geneva, W.C.C., 1964.

Another significant step had been taken within the movement during this same period. One of the popular misconceptions of the ecumenical movement in general and of the World Council in particular is that which assumes that one pattern of unity is being forced upon the churches or that they are gradually being pressurized into one institutional mode. This is a complete caricature of the facts. The World Council of Churches does not stand for any one conception of church order and the Faith and Order movement has resisted every suggestion which could have led to the conclusion that there is a World Council doctrine of the Church and a World Council pattern of church order. At the New Delhi Assembly, however, in 1961 following on action by the Faith and Order Commission there was placed on record not a description of a possible united Church but a statement of the main ingredients which would need to be discernible in any united Church. This was the widely publicized 'All-in-each-place' statement which 'in a sentence of Pauline length', as Oliver Tomkins described it, found the following formulation at New Delhi:

We believe that the unity which is both God's will and his gift to the Church is being made visible as all in each place who are baptized into Jesus Christ and confess him as Lord and Saviour are brought by the Holy Spirit into one fully committed fellowship, holding the one apostolic faith, preaching the one Gospel, breaking the one bread, joining in common prayer, and having a corporate life reaching out in witness and service to all and who at the same time are united with the whole Christian fellowship in all places and all ages in such wise that ministry and members are accepted by all, and that all can act and speak together as occasion requires for the tasks to which God calls his people.

Few World Council statements have received such widespread attention as this, or have been more closely studied whether by individual theologians, by Church authorities, local parishes and congregations, or study groups of all kinds. It provided the text of the British Council of Churches Nottingham Conference of 1964 which, under the title of 'One Church renewed for Mission', marked an exciting turning-point in the Faith and Order discussions in Britain. Months of preparatory work in local and regional groups brought the issue of mission-in-unity closer to the thought and planning of local congregations than any previous undertaking had done. The local implications of the all-in-each-place statement were discussed with a new hopefulness in the possibility of release from the stalemate which many felt had been reached in unity conversations. In particular it provided an impetus to many local developments in united work, in the sharing of resources, in united worship and to some extent in the provision of more occasions for inter-communion.

Similar consequences in the use of the New Delhi statement followed also in many other countries.

This now famous all-in-each-place statement high-lighted the significance of the Church in its local expression, an emphasis which in recent years has received considerable prominence in fresh thinking about the nature of the Church from whatever denominational or confessional standpoint the matter has been discussed. But the statement also includes a vital phrase which relates the local to the universal. It is the phrase '. . . united with the whole Christian fellowship in all places and all ages in such wise that ministry and members are accepted by all'. Here the local manifestation of unity has to be seen in the context of the Church's catholicity. In what ways, by what elements in the ordering of its life, does the local expression of unity make equally clear the universality of the Church? How can all in each place bear witness to the unity of all in all places?

For some years preceding the Uppsala Assembly this question was in the forefront of Faith and Order discussions. It was taken up by many of the churches; it entered into studies sponsored by some of the world confessional organizations, and claimed constant attention within the Faith and Order Commission and Secretariat. In the course of these deliberations two important emphases, amongst others, were constantly recurrent. The first concerned the need to think of the term catholicity from a standpoint other than that of its familiar use in any of the divided churches. The existing churches—and not only those which use the term 'catholic' in their name—all make some claim to true catholicity. They give meaning and expression to the word in their own particular histories, doctrines, and practices. Yet so long as this claim and the evidence for it are expressed only from within the divisions of the Church, there is a manifest falling short of the original and ultimate meaning of the term. In asking 'What is catholicity?', is it possible—as the Faith and Order movement has done in other matters—to press behind all the existing claims and definitions to the source of the Church's catholicity? Part at least of the answer to this was given in one of the preparatory papers for the Uppsala Assembly, which describes catholicity first and foremost as a *gift*. 'Catholicity', it was said in this paper, 'is a gift of God which requires a response of obedience. No church can claim to be catholic when it is isolated or separated from the wholeness of Christ's mission to mankind, or when it is unwilling to live by the wholeness of Christ's truth. God gives this fullness to the Church in order that men and women everywhere may find their home in its communion and that the whole of mankind may be renewed.'[9]

[9] *Drafts for Sections*, Uppsala 1968, p. 9.

In the further elaboration of this theme, especially during the Uppsala Assembly, much stress was laid on the fact that like all the gifts of grace catholicity is more than a once-upon-a-time gift: it is as living and perpetually renewed as the Holy Spirit of which it is bestowed. To be catholic is not a static condition: it is to be held within the continuous movement of grace; it involves constant growth in apprehension of the gift and in active response to its demands. Such a conception of catholicity—as was said by a Bishop of the Armenian Orthodox Church, Bishop Karekin Sarkissian of the Lebanon—'makes us question our basic assumptions about catholicity, whether in our own respective churches or in sharing in the so-called catholicity of the Church. . . . It makes us look ahead for a genuine understanding of catholicity.'

To speak of the catholicity of the Church means to speak of a vocation to be accomplished through a task entrusted to the Church, to be fulfilled by the constant sustenance and guidance of the Holy Spirit. The inward-looking and sometimes even backward-looking conception of catholicity has been radically challenged and replaced with a forward-looking perspective. Thus catholicity is no longer to be considered as a 'mark of the Church', as the traditional terminology used to describe it. . . . The catholicity of the Church is a gift of God, constantly made manifest through the operation of the Holy Spirit. . . . The Church has to become catholic when it receives from God the fullness of life and truth in Christ.[10]

This reconsideration of the meaning of catholicity led to another major shift of emphasis. The primary concern of the Faith and Order movement is the Church and in this context it is natural to discuss the subject of catholicity in exclusively ecclesiastical terms, but—as a speaker at the Bristol meeting of the Faith and Order Commission in 1967 asked—is not God's gift of catholicity offered to all the world? Is it not a movement pointing to the solidarity of all mankind, not only the unity of a 'churchly' section of it? Part of the paradoxical character of the present age lies in the fact that despite the emergence of many new and tragic divisions, some of the greatest forces in today's world are those which by their very nature are tending to obliterate differences of race, culture, and nationhood. The Uppsala Report speaks of a 'secular catholicity', the movement towards a 'single secular culture' into which technology is drawing all men. In the light of this process there are those who contend, as the Report acknowledged, that the Church 'should seek its unity through those forces in modern life, such as the struggle for racial equality, which are drawing men more closely together, and should give up its concern with patching up its own

[10] *The Uppsala Report*, p. 7.

internal disputes. To this challenge we must listen and make our response.' So the Uppsala Assembly tried to make it clear that the Church's quest for its own wholeness and unity was bound up with the contemporary tensions in the world at large. Only a Church involved in both realms can hope to find the truth about its own nature and the meaning of catholicity. As the Uppsala Report expresses it:

The same Spirit who is bringing us together in the Church does, in fact, make us more aware of the needs of the world, and of our solidarity with a creation which is 'groaning in travail together'. We cannot be isolated from the shocks and turmoils of our time as conflicts between races and nations tear apart the fabric of our common life, as developed and developing countries become more and more alienated from each other and ideologies and crusades clash in deadly struggle for survival. . . . In such a time it is the Holy Spirit who calls us to share Christ's unlimited love, to accept his condemnation of our fears and treasons, and for his sake to endure shame, oppression and apparent defeat. In the agonizing arena of contemporary history—and very often among the members of the churches—we see the work of demonic forces that battle against the rights and liberties of man, but we also see the activity of the life-giving Spirit of God. We have come to view this world of men as the place where God is already at work to make all things new and where he summons us to work with him. Engagement in such work enables us to see fresh implications in the oneness, the holiness, the catholicity and the apostolicity which in close interdependence have always characterized the authentic life of the Church.[11]

Here another new emphasis became apparent at Uppsala. It implied something like a reminting of the words 'apostolic' and 'apostolicity'. Of course these have always etymologically, practically, and spiritually signified the sending out of the disciples, the being sent of the Church, the outreaching of the Gospel, but too often they have been associated almost exclusively with the technicalities of church order as in the perennial discussion of the meaning of the apostolic succession. At Uppsala the dominant concern was with what might be called the apostolic exodus, the going out of the Church into the world. Any claim to stand within the apostolic succession must be vindicated by obvious and costly participation in the apostolic exodus. To quote Bishop Sarkissian again, 'The catholicity of the Church is taken up and carried into her apostolicity, her mission. Without such a dynamic understanding the term becomes almost an empty word, or in the best instance, a kind of holy relic to be preserved and cherished in the most treasured data of the Christian creed.'

[11] *The Uppsala Report*, p. 12.

At this point Faith and Order questions become inseparable from the total comprehensive task of the ecumenical movement in its endeavour to recover and present to the world the wholeness of the faith and the meaning and implications of the Gospel for every phase of human life. As a speaker at the Faith and Order Working Committee in 1970 said,

The question about Faith is not simply 'What message of grace can the denominations agree upon?' but 'What is the message of the Gospel for the actual controversies of mankind?', and the question about Order is no longer simply 'How can the denominations get together?' but 'How can Church unity serve the healing of mankind's divisions?' . . . 'What does Church unity, and not merely denominational realignment mean for the race problem, the poverty problem, the generation problem? How does the right and creative ordering of Christian *koinonia* eliminate the problem of man-woman relations, the problem of revolution and social justice? '

Such questions as these imply more than the assumption that by finding a way to unite the present ecclesiastical structures the world will be shown a convincing pattern of Christian unity. They compel a new approach to an understanding of the nature of that unity, that unity in diversity which is God's will for all mankind. In pressing on with this fundamental search in ever-deepening 'apostolic' involvement in the world, the churches may well find themselves confronted with new challenges not simply to their denominational separations but to some of their present assumptions about the meaning, the form, and the criteria of ecclesiastical unity.

Questions of this range and depth constituted the main theme—under the title 'The Unity of the Church and the Unity of Mankind'—of the triennial meeting of the Faith and Order Commission of the World Council held in August 1971 in Louvain where the Commission was housed in the Jesuit University at Heverlee—the first occasion in the history of the movement when the Commission has met in a Roman Catholic institution. Alongside the study of the main theme the Commission reviewed a number of ongoing studies on such subjects as Baptism, Confirmation, and the Eucharist, Ordination, Worship, and the Nature of Scriptural Authority. There was also further work on a question to which much attention has been given in recent years, namely the significance of synods and councils in the history of the Church (the 'conciliar process')[12] and the possibility that out of the present ecumenical movement there may emerge a genuinely universal council of the Church. To this question a reference will be made in a later chapter of this volume.

[12] See Appendix III(h), p. 162.

Lost Momentum?

It is now more than fifty years since the initial Faith and Order discussions in 1920. How stands the question of the organic union of the churches at this point in the story? Within the total perspectives of Christian history various achievements can be recorded.[13] Many of these have been within the same world families of churches—Lutheran or Methodist, for example; still more have embraced denominations whose differences exist within a broadly accepted tradition—such as the Reformed tradition within which Congregationalists and Presbyterians have found union relatively easy. Progress in these instances has been facilitated by a long experience of practical co-operation with mutual recognition of ministries and sacraments. While this has minimized the theological obstacles in the way of union, it has not necessarily made it easier to overcome those non-theological factors of a sociological or psychological character, or those deriving from tenacious local loyalties. Not surprisingly, the lead in many of these unions has been given in the once-called 'mission fields' of Asia and Africa where the irony of divisions arising from historical disputes in the west, seemingly irrelevant to the 'younger' churches, has been most deeply felt.

It is when the question of organic union is looked at within the total ecclesiastical scene that the achievements so far recorded can be regarded only as initial steps on a long road. Eastern and western Catholicism—the Orthodox Churches and the Roman Catholic Church—remain fundamentally separate entities, though recent decades have seen remarkable progress in relationships between the two. Since the Second Vatican Council there have been even more astonishing changes in the relationships between Rome and churches whose history reflects the great divide of the Reformation, but here the question of organic union can scarcely be said to be on the agenda as yet. As already indicated, between churches reflecting two of the main Reformation streams—Lutheran and Calvinistic—there may well be accomplished before long at least some form of formal agreement making inter-communion possible. With few exceptions the Baptist churches have tended to stand apart from most union discussions and the Pentecostal churches, whose numbers are rapidly increasing, would for the most part regard their distinctive witness and their understanding of Christian fellowship to be imperilled by any structural identity with other churches. In general, where negotiable schemes have begun with the declared aim of achieving organic union progress has been least in evidence

[13] Detailed enumerations and descriptions of these are published periodically in the *Ecumenical Review* under the title 'Surveys of Church Union Negotiations'. The last of these appeared in the July 1970 issue.

when episcopal and non-episcopal churches have sought agreement. In this respect South India broke new ground in 1947 after negotiations lasting nearly thirty years, but for more than twenty years after the inauguration of the Church of South India the Anglican communion hesitated to enter into full communion with a church which included former dioceses of an Anglican Province. It waited for the Lambeth Conference of 1968 to change this situation by declaring that 'since the Church of South India is showing itself to be an episcopally ordered Church and all its members are in communion with the bishop, we believe that the way is now open for churches of the Anglican communion to establish full communion with the Church of South India'. In North India and in Pakistan unions of episcopal and non-episcopal churches were achieved in 1970. In Ceylon (Lanka) a comparable plan which has been under negotiation for decades has yet to be implemented.

In 1965 the United Church of Jamaica and Grand Cayman brought together churches representing the Congregational, Presbyterian, and Methodist traditions, and conversations have begun between this united Church and the Disciples of Christ and the Moravians. The inauguration in 1968 of the Church of Jesus Christ in Madagascar was exceptional in its inclusion of congregations which were the result of the work of the Society of Friends. In England and Wales a union between the Congregational Church in England and Wales and the Presbyterian Church of England is nearing achievement. In Scotland union proposals between the Episcopal Church and the (Presbyterian) Church of Scotland broke down in 1959 and in England negotiations for a union between the Anglican and Methodist Churches were frustrated in 1969 through lack of a favourable vote with the required majority by the Anglican convocations. (Both the English and Scottish schemes are nevertheless still on the agenda of the Churches concerned.) In the United States of America, Canada, and South Africa recent years have seen the formulation of plans involving episcopal and non-episcopal churches on bases which seem to give more promise than hitherto of agreement on a form of episcopacy with a commonly accepted conception of the functions which might resolve the long *impasse* on this issue. In all this, what is even more significant than the stubbornness of the problem and the slow progress so far made is the persistence with which the churches are maintaining their endeavour to reach the goal.

While work continues on long-projected schemes of union and while new schemes are still being initiated in various parts of the world, the decade under review, and especially the latter part of it, has undoubtedly been marked by a loss of momentum in the pursuit of organic union. To a considerable extent this is due to increasing awareness of such factors as have already been touched upon in surveying the work of the Faith and Order movement. So many of these call for a radical reappraisement of what is meant by unity and fresh thinking concerning the nature of the Church itself. In this situation it can be a responsible reluctance which hesitates to press on with schemes which may originally have been formulated without regard to considerations now seen to be vital in the search for the true unity of the Church.

There is, however, another reason more widely—and certainly popularly—operative which has contributed to the waning of enthusiasm in regard to many long-discussed schemes of union. This arises from a deep concern about the state of the world today and the conviction that any form of institutional church is irrelevant to the most urgent needs of the age and that in consequence all discussions of ecclesiastical unity are futile. Many younger people in particular become contemptuous of what seems to them a waste of time and effort required by the intricacies of union negotiations when such energies could be better employed. How much can these ecclesiastical technicalities matter, they argue, when millions are starving, wars continue, the racial problem is unsolved, the whole fabric of ordered society is threatened with disintegration because the principles on which it is established are proving inadequate to meet either the maladies or the aspirations of mankind? Ecclesiastical fiddling while cities burn reflects a shocking failure in priorities and sensitivity. Therefore, it is urged, instead of prolonging the weary pursuit of church union let us get on with the job of translating Christian convictions and loyalties into the needs and opportunities which the world presents, especially through the many organizations outside the Church, or only slenderly related to it, which are clearly more mobile, more flexible and experimental, and more adaptable to a world in ferment. Further, in so far as this new outreach into the world can be conducted from within the churches, let the larger structures and assemblies, the hierarchies and the intractable questions of order be by-passed by local unity in action 'without tarrying for any'.

At the heart of this mood there are convictions and recognitions with which the Faith and Order movement itself is increasingly concerned, as evidenced by its current programme. What the Faith and Order movement nevertheless continues to assert is that the question before the churches and their members is not whether to press on with the unity issue or abandon it to serve the more obvious needs of the age. It is whether the world is to be served in

the power of the gospel and in the light of the Christian understanding of man and his destiny. In such service there could be no
more potent instrument than a Church which demonstrates in its
own life, as in its outreach into the world, the unifying, reconciling,
and renewing grace of God.

International Affairs

In 1968 the Chairman of the Commission of the Churches on International Affairs, Sir Kenneth Grubb, and its Director Dr. Frederick Nolde (who also had the status of an Associate General Secretary of the World Council of Churches) retired from these offices which they had held since the formation of the Commission twenty-two years earlier. In 1971 their closest senior colleague in the Commission, Dr. Elfan Rees, retired. Dr. Rees, who has been with the Commission since 1947 (after previous experience with the United Nations Relief and Works Agency), has long since been recognized as one of the leading authorities on world refugee problems.

There is scarcely any other branch of the World Council's operations which has been more affected by the character of its leadership than has this highly important Commission. This has been due not only to personal characteristics, though the three men named possess colourful attributes which enlivened many a scene. It arose primarily from the convictions, ideas, and methods of working of this team, from the circumstances of the period, and from the assumptions which had led to the creation of the Commission and determined the choice of its leaders. The Commission continues its work, structurally in a somewhat modified form, and the fact that its present Director comes from Latin America is also significant in any consideration of the interplay of persons and movements. As the close of the decade under review has marked such a turning-point in the story of this Commission it may be well to recall the origin and the main course of this ecumenical endeavour to give expression to Christian convictions in the intricate sphere of international affairs.

In 1946 I was present at a small conference in Cambridge, England. The Chairman was John Foster Dulles and two of the most influential members of the meeting were J. H. Oldham and Walter Van Kirk. Oldham was there because at that date he was still foremost among those whose counsel was sought in relation to any fresh development in the shaping of the organizations which might give expression to the ecumenical movement. Amongst his many other achievements he had been the creative and directing mind in the Oxford Conference of 1936 on Church, Community, and State, and the purpose of this conference at Cambridge was to take up again in their new context some of the recurrent fundamental questions concerning Christian responsibility within the community of nations. Walter Van Kirk was a greatly respected American church leader who, with John Foster Dulles, had also played a prominent part in the Oxford Conference. Dulles[1] and Van Kirk were respectively chairman and secretary of an organization called the Commission on a Just and Durable Peace which had been founded in 1941 under the aegis of the Federal Council of the Churches of Christ in the U.S.A. This Commission, formed before the end of the second world war was in sight, was an expression of the churches' concern that the best available Christian thinking should be concentrated on the study of some of the problems likely to confront the nations and their governments when the fighting was over. In 1942 the Commission organized at Princeton, New Jersey, an International Round Table Conference of Christian leaders in which the Americans were joined by representatives of other countries including Great Britain, Australia, and New Zealand, in an international endeavour to formulate from the Christian standpoint some guiding principles on which a 'Just and Durable' peace might be established. When the inter-governmental conference at San Francisco in 1945 was at work on the drafting of the Charter for the projected United Nations Organization, representatives of this Commission on a Just and Durable Peace, including Dulles and Nolde, were in attendance as consultants. There are features of the Charter of the United Nations, chiefly those which touch on 'human rights and fundamental freedoms', which are to a large extent the result of the work of this Commission and the American churches.

The Cambridge conference of 1946 was sponsored by two organizations—the International Missionary Council and the Provisional Committee of the World Council of Churches in Process of Formation. Alongside lay members versed in international problems there were theologians of the calibre of Reinhold Niebuhr and Emil Brunner. In the light of the tensions reflected more than twenty years later at Uppsala between the 'vertical' and 'horizontal' role of the Church it is interesting to recall an observation of Reinhold Niebuhr at Cambridge that in the search for Christian judgements amidst the ambiguities of politics 'what we have to say within the realm of the horizontal is diagonal not vertical'. 'The Christian order', Niebuhr continued in his characteristic fashion, 'is eternally

---

[1] Mr. Dulles severed his connexion with these organizations, including the Commission of the Churches on International Affairs, when he became American Secretary of State.

ambiguous pending the coming of the Kingdom of God. It must from moment to moment accept devices by which absolute Love is adjusted to the fact that people don't love one another.' Looking ahead towards likely policies of the victorious allies, especially the United States, Niebuhr added a rider to Lord Acton's dictum by saying 'Absolute power corrupts absolutely, even though it is acquired without wanting it.'

It was as a result of this Cambridge meeting in 1946 that there was formed the Commission of the Churches on International Affairs. Until the integration of the International Missionary Council and the World Council in 1961 the Commission remained under the sponsorship of these two bodies, submitting its reports and proposals to both, acting in their name as requested, but enjoying a considerable degree of autonomy. Beginning its life in the immediate post-war years two matters dominated its initial activities—the need of the refugees and the need in post-war settlements and new political alignments to safeguard human rights and fundamental freedoms, including religious liberty. The provision of resources for refugee relief was the responsibility within the World Council and the International Missionary Council of what is now called the Division of Inter-Church Aid, Refugee and World Service. The new Commission concentrated on the political aspects of the refugee problem. It made representations to governments and worked closely with the United Nations to ensure close co-operation between the agencies of United Nations and the churches in relief programmes. In the field of human rights the issue of religious liberty claimed a large part of the time and energies of the Commission. This was given in two directions. First there was the need to ensure international recognition of certain basic freedoms, and to incorporate this recognition in international and national instruments such as Declarations, Covenants, and Conventions. Here again much credit can be attributed to the Commission for the presence in the United Nations Universal Declaration on Human Rights of the Article on Religious Freedom which explicitly asserts that

Everyone has the right to freedom of thought, conscience and religion; this right includes freedom to change his religion or belief, and freedom, either alone or in community with others and in public or private, to manifest his religion or belief in preaching, practice, worship and observance.

Secondly, the Commission has taken up specific instances of the infringement of these rights and has sought by direct representations to governments and churches to remedy the situation. The fact that in the years which have followed the earlier work of the Commission in this field progress has been slow in persuading some countries to give effect to these basic human freedoms and that, alas, new tyrannies have succeeded old, has been due not to the inactivity of the Commission but to those grievous basic facts that men do not love one another and that absolute power corrupts absolutely.

The close relationship with the emerging United Nations which was an obvious need when the Commission of the Churches on International Affairs was formed has been maintained through the years. It is in permanent contact with the Economic and Social Council and its subsidiary commissions, notably with the Commission on Human Rights. It has the same consultative status with the Food and Agriculture Organization, the International Labour Office, the United Nations Educational, Scientific, and Cultural Organization and the United Nations Children's Fund and, through the Christian Medical Commission with the World Health Organization. It also has very close working relationships with the United Nations High Commissioner for Refugees, the Intergovernmental Committee for European Migration, and the United Nations Relief and Works Agency for Palestine Refugees. During sessions of the United Nations Assembly officers of the Commission are in regular attendance and for many years each delegate to the Assembly has received from the Commission a set of notes based on the agenda for the session. These include extracts from statements by the churches on matters to be discussed and they set out the views of the Commission or of the World Council where these have been formulated in relation to specific agenda items. By way of illustration, the notes distributed through this procedure to delegates attending the twenty-fifth session of the General Assembly in 1970 touched on more than fifty agenda items. Considerable data was provided on such matters as *apartheid* in South Africa, Vietnam ('a symbol for our time of the misery of a developing people caught in a world conflict . . . an example of the tragedy to which unilateral intervention of a great power can lead'), and the proposed International Convention on the Elimination of All Forms of Religious Intolerance.

In the preamble to nearly fifty pages of these notes there is a long statement by the Commission referring to the twenty-fifth anniversary of United Nations. This speaks of 'mounting dangers to the hopes' which 'gave birth to the United Nations'. 'It is threatened by a creeping paralysis from the indifference of peoples and the self-regard of states. . . . Resolutions are adopted without regard to their implementation as a kind of substitute for action; resolutions are adopted for propaganda effect without regard for the organization.

Even unanimous resolutions of the Security Council are not en-
forced.' Over against this sombre note in the birthday greeting
there is a grateful acknowledgement of the main achievements
of United Nations, especially those which have 'helped one-third of
mankind on their march to statehood', done so much in the care of
refugees, migrants, and children, and made many advances in the
economic and social field 'essential to the pursuit of justice and co-
operation'. This was followed by an urgent plea to the member
states to fulfil their obligations and equip United Nations for its
great and still much-needed task. The statement closes with an
appeal to the churches for the 'greater attention, study and critical
support' which United Nations should command and adds that:

in their own field the churches need to work out a new theological analysis and critique of power, based on Christian beliefs and insights but finding expression in concrete judgements on events and policies and concrete
proposals for change in the existing international, political and economic
system and in the ethical presuppositions on which it rests.

The Commission and its officers have devoted almost continuous
attention through the years to issues of war and peace. They have
been in attendance at successive Disarmament Conferences in
Geneva and have been able to draw on the scientific and political
expertise of Christian laymen as advisers when making representations on such matters as the planning or control of nuclear weapons.
On occasion officers of the Commission have met with selected
governmental delegates to the Disarmament Conferences and have
sought to win agreement to policies which would remove the threat
of atomic war and harness the use of atomic power to peaceful ends.
Alongside the endeavour to reduce the threat of war and the means
to wage it there have been interventions in existing conflicts—as in
Korea, Cyprus and Vietnam—not only through public declarations
and appeals but by personal representations to the leaders of warring
states. If only modest success—or none that is immediately apparent
—has attended such missions, at least a constructive and reconciling
Christian witness has been attempted.

The Commission has operated through a small Executive Committee and its very small but expert staff, making consultative use
of the Commissioners. The majority of these are lay folk with
experience in various aspects of national and international policy
making. In all, they represent a highly qualified cadre of resource
persons of all nationalities and confessions, some of whom have been
called upon for a great deal of service not only as advisers but in
the fulfilment of particular assignments. While the churches of
which these people are members are consulted before their appoint-

ment as commissioners is ratified a primary consideration in their selection is the nature of their experience and their expertise in some feature of the Commission's tasks. The officers of the Commission have always applauded, and often made use of William Temple's saying that 'If I fell into a canal I would much prefer to see on the bank a burglar who could swim than an archbishop who could not.' While the analogy need not be pressed too far, especially as the Commission includes no archbishop, competence in a highly technical realm is regarded as a *sine qua non* of appointment to a (voluntary and unpaid) commissionership.

Like almost every other department of the World Council's work the Commission of the Churches on International Affairs illustrates the enormous change in the character of relationships with the Roman Catholic Church during recent years. When the decision to create the Commission was taken in 1946, much thought was given to the possibility of inviting Roman Catholic participation at the outset. The decision went against this on grounds which included 'such obstacles as differing stances towards Communist societies, matters of religious freedom, and the pattern and forms of Vatican diplomacy'.[2] As in other matters there were personal contacts which tempered the absence of formal relationships and in connexion with particular policies and programmes, as for example work on the problem of refugees and migrants, there developed a good deal of co-operation. It was not, however, until 1965 that, with the decision to create the Joint Working Group between the World Council and the Vatican, more formal co-operation in international affairs became possible. Since then some useful contacts have been made with the Pontifical Commission on Justice and Peace.

The aims of the Commission of the Churches on International Affairs as formulated in its Constitution include that of serving as 'an organ in formulating the Christian mind on world issues and in bringing that mind effectively to bear upon such issues'. Is there, in fact, 'a Christian mind' on world issues? On what particular issues touching national and international policies is it possible to say in the name of world-wide Christian opinion 'This is the Christian view. This is the unanimous judgement of the churches'? Strictly speaking there are few, if any, such matters. For example, in general terms there is universal Christian condemnation of war. The first Assembly of the World Council declared that 'War as a method of settling disputes is incompatible with the teaching and example of our Lord Jesus Christ. The part which war plays in our present international life is a sin against God and a degradation of man.'

[2] O. Frederick Nolde in *The Ecumenical Advance*, London, SPCK, 1970, p. 266.

With slight variations of form these convictions have since been reiterated and endorsed by many churches. Yet beyond this general assertion the World Council, as in this same declaration at Amsterdam, recognizes the existence of a large body of Christian opinion which holds that 'in the absence of impartial supra-national institutions military action is the ultimate sanction of the rule of law'. To take another example, on the racial issue there is a widespread agreement with the statement of the second Assembly of the World Council that 'any form of segregation based on race, colour or ethnic origin is contrary to the Gospel and is incompatible with the Christian doctrine of man and the nature of the Church of Christ'. Again, however, it is not only the existence of the Dutch Reformed Church of South Africa which provides stubborn evidence of the lack of unanimity amongst Christians on this issue. What organization can really 'formulate the Christian mind' on such matters and 'bring that mind effectively to bear upon them'? The World Council of Churches or the Commission of the Churches on International Affairs or the Vatican can formulate judgements which are widely and generally held within a particular group of churches or within a distinctive part of the Christian community, but can any of these authorities claim a more representative status than this for their pronouncements?

At the Cambridge Conference in 1946 Dr. Visser 't Hooft asked 'Is there really a place for an ecumenical church expression of the Christian conscience?' Not even in one of their more exuberant moments have the officers of the Commission answered this question by saying, 'Yes, and we are it.' At most they would have contended that the Commission is endeavouring to contribute to the process of answering the question. This contribution is two-fold. First it seeks to inform and challenge 'the Christian conscience' with relevant and reliable data. Secondly, it offers an instrument through which an informed Christian conscience can make its witness more effective on matters vital to the integrity and fidelity of the Church universal. The making of this two-fold contribution remains a continuing endeavour rather than an accomplished task.

In 1946 more than half of the sixty members of the Cambridge Conference came from Anglo-Saxon lands. There were only two people present from Eastern Europe and only one 'younger' churchman. From the beginning the officers of the Commission were keenly aware of the need to ensure that the organization should be more genuinely worldwide not only in numerical representation but in its ability to reflect the experience and thought of Christians in all parts of the world. By 1970 about half of the seventy Commissioners came from Western Europe and the United States of

America and the other half were from Eastern Europe, the Middle East, Asia and Africa. For some years after 1946, however, the process of achieving a well-balanced representation was slow, and since the most immediate and urgent concerns of the Commission were those arising from the war and its aftermath either European problems or problems in relation to which the former allied nations carried special responsibility tended to dominate the scene. Moreover, while the principal officers of the Commission, American and British, had long since learned to 'look at big maps' and were by no means addicted to thinking simply as Americans or British, it was almost inevitable that underlying their approach to many issues there were tacit assumptions more reflective of western than of eastern thought and feeling. The principal officers were men who knew their way around the corridors of power in the American State Department, the British Foreign Office or United Nations, and it would have been very surprising if even with their rare gift of detachment and objectivity they did not occasionally resemble their civil service friends or produce memoranda that would have read as acceptably as leading articles in the London or New York *Times* as in the minutes of a World Council meeting.

Further, in the creation and initial stages of this twenty-year endeavour to 'formulate the Christian mind' on international affairs— or at least contribute to its formulation—certain classic convictions and assumptions bound up with that elusive but far from non-existent entity once called Christendom had not in the main been as radically assailed as they have in more recent years. There were tacit agreements concerning the reality and universality of 'natural law', the significance of 'law and order' and even the meaning of such concepts as justice and freedom. Deeper than diversities of definition in these matters there lay certain common acceptances in the 'civilized' mind. The 'Christian' mind could start with these. On an historic occasion in the British House of Commons in the nineteenth century a Government spokesman was challenged to define 'the pound sterling'. After many hesitancies and false starts the Minister could only stammer 'Any gentleman knows what the pound sterling is.' Heirs of the fundamental thought and assumptions of western Christendom might have retaliated to certain obstinate questions even well into the present century by contending that any thoughtful Christian knows what the terms justice, freedom, and peace really signify. Today, the climate of thought in the world is too harsh and fundamentally sceptical for any of these assumptions to be enjoyed without radical challenge.

One of the attempted but abandoned undertakings of the Commission of the Churches on International Affairs was the promotion

soon after the second Assembly of the World Council of a study on
'A Christian approach to an international ethos'. While limited
resources and the pressure of the other tasks contributed to the defeat of this endeavour there was also the recognition that midway
in this tumultuous twentieth century some of the most vital factors
needed in such a study—philosophical and sociological as well as
theological and political—were scarcely yet accessible. Meantime,
'the Christian mind' in relation to temporal affairs which presuppose fundamental agreement in these areas is still on pilgrimage.
In the process neither the Christian mind nor the Christian heart
abandons responsibility towards the world of nations and the search
amidst the ambiguities of politics for a 'just' international order. As
Reinhold Niebuhr said at that historic Cambridge conference
twenty-five years ago, 'The Christian conscience beguiles that world
nearer the Kingdom by its vision of the City of God.'

The Training of the Ministry

When the International Missionary Council at Jerusalem in 1928
formulated priorities for the Christian world mission in the years
ahead, great prominence was given to the critical task of training
men and women for indigenous Christian leadership. 'Leadership',
it said, 'must be self-giving, free, independent, and purposeful.'

In attempts to equip men and women for service, often in the past
violence has been done by formal and ill-adapted foreign educational
methods and processes. The problem is the training of leaders for a living
organism. The future leaders of the indigenous churches will be men and
women called from home, school and church who will be true to the
social genius of other people, who will retain the fine zest of spiritual
vigour and who are free personalities. Just as truly will they be those
who have had the opportunity of availing themselves of all those elements
in the Christian heritage which can enrich and empower for ever en-
larging service.

It is quite possible that the training centre which will render this kind
of service for the Church is yet to arise. The curriculum and training
method appropriate to such an institution are perhaps yet to be discovered. Certainly experiments made in recent years in higher education
among the older churches and having to do with the constant alternation
between study and actual life situations ought to be reckoned with and
may point the way.

In the meantime the theological colleges and bible training schools need
to be studied and reappraised. Curricula and teaching staff should be
adjusted in the direction of achieving such a training ideal.[3]

Ten years later the Tambaran meeting of the Council declared

[3] Report of the International Missionary Council, Jerusalem, 1928,
Vol. III, pp. 213f.

It is our conviction that the present condition of theological education is one of the greatest weaknesses in the whole Christian enterprise, and that no great improvement can be expected until churches and mission boards pay far greater attention to this work, particularly to the need for co-operative and united effort, and contribute more largely in funds and personnel in order that it may be effectively carried out.[4]

The anxiety expressed in such declarations as these was related to the character and quality of the training being provided, not only to the need for increasing its quantity. How relevant were generally accepted methods of ministerial training, including the teaching of theology, to the needs of emerging churches in Asia and Africa? What degree of priority were churches and mission boards giving to the training of an indigenous ministry and to the search for the most appropriate methods of training? Questions of this kind were pressed with renewed vigour after Tambaram by the International Missionary Council and by some of the national Christian councils in its membership. India led the way with the publication in 1945 of *The Christian Minister in India*[5]—a detailed survey and appraisal, under the auspices of the National Christian Council, of the existing colleges and seminaries. This was followed a year later by another study under the same auspices of what the process of formulating an 'indigenous' theology might require and imply.[6] These two studies were the fruit of several years' work in which the colleges themselves had participated and much was done in subsequent years to implement the findings of the reports. Between 1950 and 1953 the International Missionary Council initiated comparable studies in Africa. Three teams visited almost all the training institutions in all the territories south of the Sahara. They discussed with African ministers and their teachers the role of the ministry in changing Africa and the meaning of theology in relation to it.

Theology is not simply a subject that can be taught, studied and discussed in academic terms [said the report of one of these surveys]. It is nothing less than the central Christian message addressed to the situation in which the church finds itself. It is an affirmation and unfolding of the Word in relation to the present moment in history and the circumstances amidst which it is spoken. . . . A fundamental problem for the theological teacher is that of quickening in his students (and always renewing for himself) the capacity to understand theologically the real and fateful

---

[4] *Report of the International Missionary Council*, Jerusalem, 1928, Vol. IV, p. 211.
[5] C. W. Ranson, *The Christian Minister in India; his vocation and training*, London, Lutterworth Press, 1945.
[6] Marcus Ward, *Our Theological Task in India*, Madras, Christian Literature Society for India, 1946.

encounter between Christianity and paganism as this is lived out and fought out at the personal level.[7]

These far-ranging investigations and discussions in India and Africa prompted many new local initiatives and met with an encouraging response from mission boards. They also provided some of the most convincing data on which a successful appeal for financial assistance in the cause of theological training was made by the International Missionary Council to John D. Rockefeller Jr. of the Sealantic Fund. Mr. Rockefeller made a challenge offer to the Council of two million dollars on condition that an equivalent amount was contributed by the mission boards over and above their existing commitments. This condition was met and at its meeting in Ghana in 1958 the International Missionary Council established a Theological Education Fund which has proved to be the largest single undertaking conducted by the Council, whether in its original form or as an integral part of the World Council of Churches. Although the Fund has been operating since 1958 and is now working on a programme which is not expected to terminate before 1976 it was never assumed that it would constitute a permanent organization for the financing of theological schools and colleges. Its resources have always been devoted to stimulating initiatives and evoking support from within the churches and mission agencies concerned. The original challenge gift produced not only the two million dollars required from the mission boards but led to the contribution of approximately another four million dollars from churches, councils of churches, and mission agencies throughout the world. It is expected that something like a further three million dollars will be needed from the same sources to complete the project programme up to 1976.

In the first phase of the Fund's operations (1958 to 1960) attention was focused on the need for strengthening certain existing key institutions. Twelve major grants of approximately $100,000 each were allocated to centres of training in Asia, Africa, and Latin America. These grants assisted the formation of united theological colleges in Korea, Madagascar, the West Indies, South India, South West Africa, and Mexico. In the Middle East both the Coptic Orthodox Theological College in Cairo and the Near East School of Theology were helped. In addition to these substantial grants a number of smaller experimental projects were assisted in Central Africa, Guatemala, and Chile. Another priority in the purposes of

[7] The three reports of these surveys were made the basis of B. G. M. Sundkler's comprehensive study *The Christian Ministry in Africa*, London, Lutterworth Press, 1960.

the Fund was the strengthening of libraries and the provision of theological textbooks in the languages of the area where they were to be used. Over three hundred libraries were aided in this first period and by the end of 1969 more than four hundred textbooks, commentaries, and Bible dictionaries had been produced in twenty-seven languages. All this work is, of course, done through local agencies. In 1960 and 1968 two massive annotated bibliographies for the use of libraries were also published and regional directories of theological schools have been produced.

A review of the work and policy of the Fund in 1963 led to some new emphases. Some 250 grants were made towards experimental projects which gave promise of leading to 'a real encounter between the student and the Gospel in terms of his own forms of thought and culture and to a living dialogue between the Church and its environment'. Increased attention was also given to the need for strengthening the indigenous staffs of seminaries and encouraging research and post-graduate study by faculty members. Associations of theological schools, mainly on a regional basis, were promoted and assisted. These provide occasions for the sharing of information and experience and for the study of common problems in relation to the ministry, its recruiting and training. The publication of locally or regionally produced journals of theological studies has also been encouraged and assisted.

In 1968 and 1969 a further reappraisal of the work of the Fund was made by a small advisory group which included members from Japan, India, Latin America, Africa, the United States, and Great Britain. While recognizing the immense progress in the sphere of theological education since the lamentations recorded at Jerusalem 1928 and Tambaram 1938, and acknowledging the part played by the Theological Education Fund in this achievement, a sobering note reappears in the course of this latest appraisal. 'For the most part,' says the report, 'theological education has not yet found truly indigenous expression. In Asia, Africa, and Latin America it reflects too often European and American patterns of thought.' This long-standing weakness is seen to be more grave in the context of the contemporary cultural crisis.

Theological education takes place in a specific cultural and religious context. These local cultural situations are today characterized by the interaction between the traditional cultural and religious heritage and a universal technological civilization which penetrates into all parts of the world. The result is generally not the disappearance of the ancient culture and religion but rather its renaissance and transformation. Theological education, in order to be effective, must be fully aware of this dialectic between universal technological civilization and local cultural situations.

Speaking of the necessary dialogue between Christianity and other faiths and the tasks of the Christian ministry in relation to it the report says:

The real dialogue between Christianity and other faiths can only be carried out by those who have entered deeply into the cultural problems of the area concerned and participate actively in the task of expressing the faith in such a way that it can act as a leaven within the local cultural situation. This requires patient study of the local culture and society for the development of a theology which, with imagination and open-mindedness, combines faithfulness to the revealed truth with an awareness of the manner in which contemporary life is expressed.

The determining policy of the Theological Education Fund in the period envisaged as culminating in 1976 was described by the Advisory Group as that of helping the churches 'to find a form and content of the ministry for our time so that the Gospel may be expressed in response to the call of God with regard to (a) the urgent issues of human development and social justice, (b) the dialectic between a universal technological civilization and local cultural situations, and (c) the widespread crisis of faith and the search for meaning'. Perhaps the most important phrase in this policy statement is 'the widespread crisis of faith and the search for meaning'. Amplifying this the Advisory Group said:

Theological education is today deeply affected by the widespread calling in question of traditional expressions of the faith, of established church structures and of customary methods of education. This is true all over the world and not only in those areas where the Theological Education Fund has been at work. It would seem that underlying this is, on the one hand a crisis of faith, and on the other a new search for meaning. We find indeed among students in the theological schools a great uncertainty about the content of the Christian faith and about the mission of the Church, but we find at the same time that many of them are eagerly looking for meaningful answers to the fundamental questions of life. Many students now enter theological schools without a clear vocation to become ministers and to serve the Church. Many come with the hope that the study of theology will help them to find a sense of direction for their life.

The status of the Theological Education Fund within the World Council of Churches is that of a 'sponsored agency' of the Commission on World Mission and Evangelism. As such, and in line with its original objectives as an agency of the former International Missionary Council, its field of concern and action lies outside Europe and North America. Its attention and resources are directed to the specially critical needs of the churches in Asia, Africa, Latin America, the Caribbean, and the South Pacific. What has been increasingly clear, however, is that such fundamental questions and needs as the Fund's operations have exposed outside Europe and North America are becoming daily more urgent in the lands of the historic 'sending churches'. What the Mexico meeting of the Commission on World Mission and Evangelism in 1963 described as 'the mission to six continents' applies to the need for reform, renewal, and relevance in a concept of Christian ministry all the world over. Here again one feature of the work of the World Council of Churches directed to part of the world is seen to be integral to the total ecumenical task as needed in all the world.

Education

The late nineteenth and early twentieth centuries saw the rise of a number of international Christian organizations which, in varying degrees, were expressions of the ecumenical movement and directly or indirectly helped to prepare the ground for the formation of a World Council of Churches. Much earlier, of course, the world missionary movement, the Bible societies, and the Christian literature societies had already crossed national and denominational frontiers and fostered a concern for unity in the interests of worldwide Christian witness. None of these movements was indifferent to the need to nurture new generations in the faith and therefore all were to some extent concerned with education. This involvement was in two directions. First, in the provision of the means of a general education, as in the vast network of schools, colleges, and universities founded or promoted under missionary auspices; secondly, in the concern for the systematic training of young people in Christian faith and practice. The later nineteenth- and twentieth-century world movements included some which were primarily directed towards young people and especially students. The YMCA and YWCA worked on a wider mandate than that concerned with the student world alone, but they have always included the needs of students within their activities. The Student Christian Movements, federated in the World Student Christian Federation, have concentrated not only on student activities but on the meaning and instruments of education. There has been considerable interlocking between all these organizations, especially in their leadership and sources of support, and with the formation of the World Council of Churches provision was made in the Council's constitution for the participation of fraternal delegates from such bodies. This facility has been well used and practical co-operation has been close.

In 1971 the integration with the World Council of another of these movements was accomplished. This was the World Council of Christian Education. As early as 1889 there was held a World Sunday School Convention, the precursor of a number of international

gatherings concerned with Sunday School work. These prepared
the way for the formation in 1907 of the World Sunday School
Association. Organizationally the member units of this Association
were national bodies such as the Sunday School Unions or Associations which had been built up in Europe and the United States and
which had spread to many countries in Asia and Africa. In 1947 the
name of the Association was changed to that of the World Council
of Christian Education, in recognition that the work of the Association and that of its member units now covered a wider age group
than that of children and had to do with processes of education
going far beyond the traditional Sunday Schools. It was concerned
not only with nurture in the Christian faith but with the fundamental question 'What *is* education in the light of the Christian
understanding of the meaning of life and the nature and destiny of
man?'

From the inception of the World Council of Churches this educational movement has been closely related in practice to the World
Council. The World Council of Christian Education is a member,
with the World Council, of the World Christian Youth Commission
and it has been much involved in the policies and programmes of
the Laity Department and Youth Department of the World Council.
The logic of this development, combined with a common concern
for the whole field of education, has pointed to the wisdom of
finding a place within the structure of the World Council for the
expanding work of its kindred body. In 1962 both Councils agreed
to the formation of a Joint Study Commission on Education, which
was given a threefold task. First,

To consider in the light of the Christian faith the nature and function of
education in our changing societies, to examine the nature of the
churches' responsibility in and for education, and to work towards the
formulation of a common theological understanding of education.

Secondly,

to make recommendations to the two sponsoring bodies on ways of assisting the churches in the fulfilment of their responsibilities in general
education and to suggest the priorities to which the organizations should
address themselves.

Thirdly,

to make sample studies of the present practices of the churches in the
nurture and training of their members, to ascertain what are the most
pressing needs and to suggest how the two organizations might be of
assistance to the churches in developing new lines of approach to this
task.

The Commission was a high-powered body composed of educational experts—theorists, specialists, and general practitioners from many different countries, east and west. It set up working parties, study conferences, and research projects. It held consultations with Roman Catholic educationists and with such organizations as UNESCO. Its report, the product of several years' work, was a significant contribution to the international and inter-cultural discussion of educational theory and practice, as well as a keen critique of the achievements and limitations of the churches' educational work. It was animated throughout by a sense of the contemporary cultural crisis and by what it termed the current 'explosion in education . . . part of the more frequently recognized explosions in knowledge, in technology, in population and in expectations'. The Commission was concerned not only with the vastly expanded programmes of formal education being promoted in almost every country. It saw that the explosion is resulting in a tumultuous enlargement of an education which has 'broken out of the schoolroom'. An immense array of new educating agencies has now to be reckoned with. 'The armies and navies of the world have become the educators of whole generations.' Trade unions, business, and industry have entered the educational field. Youth clubs, cinema clubs, political clubs are all instruments of education, and as the report says, outreaching and out-racing all the others there are the mass media of communication operating 'at their own high pitch and furious tempo' and suggesting values and goals, attitudes and loyalties. Alongside all this the report took account of the activities of 'those who would if they could—and will if they can—explode the explosion. Their reasons are a revolutionary dissatisfaction with the goals enunciated by most educators, distrust of the values commonly invoked, defiance of a system which ever more efficiently instructs the new generation in means that they see leading straight to inhuman ends: unendurable iniquities among men, intolerable narrowing of human possibilities, blasphemous vulgarisations of spirit.'

The report of this Commission was presented to the Uppsala Assembly in one of its more scintillating sessions and it became clear that while at some point the World Council would need to resist the insistent demands from all quarters to add yet more items to its already overloaded programme, in this field of education there was an inescapable obligation to attempt far more than hitherto. The immediate result was the establishment within the Council of an Office of Education, jointly directed and financed by the World Council of Churches and the World Council of Christian Education. This was accompanied by the launching on the same joint basis of an Education Renewal Fund, which aimed at securing two million dollars a year for three years 'to encourage renewal and reform of education in the churches and in society'. The programme agreed upon was divided into two parts—one for the support of existing work and the other for sponsoring new experiments. The first of these included:

(a) strengthening the indigenous leadership of lay academies, education programmes and youth activities focusing on educational reform.
(b) scholarships and travel subsidies for educators, especially from areas of greatest need;
(c) the development of models and pilot projects to encourage the necessary adaptation to changing situations.

Amongst the new experiments envisaged were

(a) educational services to special groups such as: illiterate and semi-illiterate youth; girls and women denied essential rights; theological students and young pastors in view of the specific crises of their profession; and minorities fighting for equal rights;
(b) evaluation and development of leadership in situations of educational and social crisis;
(c) a special study process on contemporary morality, on conscience and conscience-formation, with a view to the necessary renewal of moral education for a life in the emergent world society.

It is difficult not to append to aspirations so framed the comment 'And how?' This, in fact, is the task on which the staffs and committees of both the World Council of Churches and the World Council of Christian Education are working. By 1970 about two-thirds of the first million dollars had been secured for the Education Renewal Fund and projects submitted from various parts of the world for assistance under the terms of the fund were being sifted. Meantime this steady growth in administrative co-operation between the two Councils, as well as in their formulation of common policies, led in 1971 to a decision that the World Council of Christian Education should become an integral part of the World Council of Churches, operating within a unit now known as that of Education and Communication.

Christian Literature

The slogan 'Feed the minds' as now used in campaigns for promoting the production and distribution of Christian literature is of fairly recent origin but the injunction and the organization of a worldwide Christian response to it belong to the earlier stages of the ecumenical movement. Concurrently with the missionary awakening of the eighteenth and nineteenth centuries, there emerged a number of literature producing agencies concerned with the worldwide witness of the Church. In Britain the Society for Promoting Christian Knowledge was formed as early as 1698, and the United Society for Christian Literature appeared in its original form as the Religious Tract Society in 1799. Both of these organizations set up agencies in various parts of the world. They worked closely with the missionary societies and with the British and Foreign Bible Society, which concentrated on the translation and circulation of the Scriptures as the most fundamental body of literature needed for the nurture of Christians. Soon after the World Missionary Conference at Edinburgh in 1910 the Continuation Committee of the Conference (the precursor of the International Missionary Council) set up an International Committee on Christian Literature through which, during the next few decades, there was a large expansion in the production and distribution of books in many languages. Much attention was given to specialized needs as in relation to the Muslim world and in many national Christian Councils active literature departments were established with the help of the International Missionary Council.

In line with these earlier endeavours after the integration of the International Missionary Council and the World Council of Churches the Commission on World Mission and Evangelism decided in 1963 to establish a Christian Literature Fund analogous to the Theological Education Fund. Its declared purpose was 'to assist projects and programmes developed by Christian literature agencies for which they and their supporting bodies accept full responsibility and which (a) give promise of achievement superior in quality and effectiveness to what already exists; (b) are assured by responsible agencies of a reasonable measure of local support; and (c) will be either fully supported without aid from the Fund after a reasonable period not exceeding five years or brought to a fruitful completion within the same period.' Approximately one-third of the fund was to be earmarked for the training of writers, editors, printers, publishers, and booksellers in the countries of greatest need. A five-year programme was adopted on an anticipated budget of three million dollars. By the end of this first period well over two and a half million dollars had been contributed by the churches and missionary agencies and allocated to various projects in Asia, Africa, the Middle East, Latin America, and the South Pacific. After a review of this first-year programme it was decided to continue the operation until 1975 in the expectation that the fund would then become a permanent part of the World Council's service. The name of the fund was changed to that of the Agency for Christian Literature Development and in a restatement of its functions emphasis was placed on the needs (a) 'to promote significant advance in the provision of literature addressed with Christian concern to man in his total situation and speaking the language of contemporary society; and (b) to continue the shift of decision-making from the supporting agencies of the west to Asia, Africa and Latin America.' A further significant step at this time was the decision that the new agency should work in close collaboration with the World Association for Christian Communication. This Association, which began its life as the World Association for Christian Broadcasting, is an autonomous organization which was formed in 1963. Its purpose is to provide an international forum, clearing-house and service agency for the churches in furthering the enormous and urgent task of relating Christian witness to the new techniques of communication especially in the mass media.

Medical Service

Medical missions have always made the most immediate appeal to Christian generosity and even to a public otherwise unsympathetic to missions and indifferent to the Gospel. At the receiving end some of the most poignant and urgent of human needs have been met by the dedication of missionary doctors and nurses. This ministry has also contributed to the building up of indigenous medical services and it has always demonstrated in more than words the fact that Christianity teaches us to care.

As with the educational and literature work of missions, medicine is an area in which co-operation across denominational frontiers has been a natural and necessary process from early days. Hospitals and medical schools in Asia and Africa have in the most significant instances been joint undertakings. In many countries there have resulted national professional associations concerned with the more than local approach to policy-making and action. Such national associations have developed contacts with one another and the world meetings of the International Missionary Council were nearly always accompanied by international conferences on medical policy and practice as seen from the Christian standpoint.

Medical service continues to form a vital part of the worldwide mission of the Church, but the term 'medical missions', though still applicable to one of the most urgent and appealing aspects of the work of the churches' missionary agencies, has to be read within a more complex and more demanding situation than once appeared to exist. Although the gulf between the haves and the have-nots in the availability of medical skills is still in many parts of the world appalling, indigenous health services exist on varying scales in most countries. Government hospitals and public health services provide the necessary framework within which voluntary agencies need to fashion their policies and deploy their resources to the best advantage. Advances in all the technological aspects of medicine and public health require standards in building and equipment as well as in professional competence which can prove costly in the extreme. Preventive medicine assumes an increasingly vital role; essential research and experiment make costly demands, and many new developments—as in transplant surgery and long-term resuscitation procedures—pose new ethical questions vital to any Christian appraisal of the ends and means of science in relation to persons.

Such considerations as these led in 1968 to the setting up within the World Council of Churches of a Christian Medical Commission designed

(1) to promote the more effective use of resources for medical work through the establishment of structures for joint planning and action (a) between the churches themselves, whether WCC member churches or not, and (b) between the churches collectively, other voluntary agencies and the government;
(2) to undertake and encourage the study of the nature of the Christian ministry of healing and the problems which confront it in a changing world.

The phrase 'whether WCC members or not' in the first of the above paragraphs is important. In addition to anticipating a very wide range of co-operation from the churches, it was decided at the outset that the Commission should seek the most effective possible relationships with appropriate agencies of the United Nations. The objectives towards which the activities of the Commission were to be directed included support for the establishment of joint training programmes, facilities for the exchange of personnel, and the development of a common strategy in the co-operation between voluntary agencies and government programmes. The Commission also aimed at becoming an international centre of information on existing health and medical programmes and on methods of administration in medical institutions.

During the first three years of the Commission's activities, in addition to meeting specific requests from many countries for assistance and advice a detailed survey was made in eighteen different countries of church-related medical institutions. Some disturbing conclusions were drawn from this survey. It was reckoned that 95 per cent of the churches' medical activities were concentrated on curative service in hospitals or clinics. Very little was being done to promote health or to prevent disease, yet even in relation to curative needs the combined resources of governments and churches in the developing countries made hospital services accessible only to about 15 per cent of the population. Further, despite the co-operation of earlier years in the establishment of some of the principal medical schools and hospitals, there appeared little evidence of a co-ordinated strategy in much of the medical work still being maintained by the churches The consequence was to be seen in wasteful overlapping and duplication in the use of resources that are necessarily limited. In the light of such facts as these and the need which churches and missions now readily acknowledge for assistance in reshaping their medical policies and programmes, the Central Committee of the World Council in 1971 authorized a continuation of the work of the Commission with some important new recommendations. The most significant of these concerned the possibility of official Roman Catholic representation in the membership of the Commission. This was encouraged by the fact that already in the initial work of the Commission some National Episcopal Conferences and missionary institutes of the Roman Catholic Church had raised the question of possible joint planning in medical work. These approaches had led to the setting up of a joint exploratory committee by the Vatican Secretariat for Promoting Christian Unity and the World Council of Churches. This committee is now exploring ways and means not only of maintaining this collaboration but of promoting a joint study of some of the fundamental presuppositions of Christian healing and the wholeness of men.

And so on—
Since the second Assembly of the World Council of Churches the administration has included a division bearing the name of the Division of Ecumenical Action. The name is not altogether apt, for it may seem to imply either that the rest of the organization is more ecumenically vocal than active or that ecumenical action is conceived only in terms of the programmes of this particular segment of the Council. Neither of these implications was ever intended. The division's chief concern has been with the interpretation of the significance of the ecumenical movement in general, and the World Council in particular, for 'real-life' situations, especially at the local level. This aim was redefined at the Uppsala Assembly:

to stir up and equip all of God's people for ecumenical understanding, active engagement in renewing the life of the churches and participation in God's work in a changing world.

This is an aim of infinite scope and the contribution of the Division to its achievement has mainly been pursued in three or four directions. These have included a very vigorous Youth Department working in close association with other world youth organizations and with the youth departments of the churches; the Department on the Work of the Laity—not simply lay-service within the Church but the key role of Christian men and women in every area of life; a Department on the Co-operation of Men and Women in Church, Family and Society (not 'women's work' or even 'women's rights' mainly but the responsibility resting on both sexes for working out the true meaning of partnership in living); and Education. This last function has had to do with both education as Christian nurture and education in the more generally-accepted scope of the term. In this last area the department has carried the main responsibility for co-operation with the World Council of Christian Education and the negotiations concerning its integration with the World Council of Churches.

A unique institution, coming formally within the range of this department, is the famous Ecumenical Institute at Bossey which functions as a Graduate School of the University of Geneva and as a wonderfully influential residential and tutorial centre for 'frontier' studies. Residential courses of short or long duration are provided year by year in a form which makes possible (in three languages with simultaneous translation) intensive consultations and discussions on the implications of the Christian faith for men and women involved in the professions, in science, industry, politics, law, and education as well as in the direct service of the Church. The Ecumenical Institute is an autonomous institution with its own international Board of Governors, but its work lies at the heart of the World Council's diversity of concerns and aims. Few people, if any, can have attended one of Bossey's courses or conferences and have left this delectable spot just outside Geneva without discovering in the most moving fashion what the term 'ecumenical experience' signifies.

Advisory or Executive?

The primary responsibilities of the World Council of Churches are consultative and advisory, not executive. In its Constitution the Council is authorized 'to *facilitate* common action by the churches . . . to *promote* co-operation and study . . . to *support* churches in their worldwide missionary and evangelistic task'. The Council is to *facilitate, promote, support* action by the bodies which are properly responsible for action, namely the churches. In the constitutional definition of the Council's authority the same emphasis is made. 'The World Council shall *offer counsel* and *provide opportunity* of united action. . . . It may take action on behalf of constituent churches *in such matters as one or more of them shall commit to it.* . . . The World Council shall not legislate for the churches; nor shall it *act for them* in any manner except as indicated above [in the phrases quoted] or *as may be specified by the constituent churches.'*

It was my privilege between 1948 and 1969 to attend not only the four Assemblies of the Council but all the annual meetings of its Central Committee, most of its twice-yearly Executive Committees and innumerable departmental committees. I had also been present at the meetings of the Council's Provisional Committee in the two years preceding its full inauguration in 1948. During this period the main principles which were to determine the character of the Council were being formulated. All through these experiences I was made aware of the sensitivity of the Council's leaders, its committee members and the representatives of the member churches in regard to the distinction between an organization acting in its own right and one whose principal role was to *facilitate* or *support* action by others. The fear of creating a so-called 'super-church' was the fear not only of the opponents of the movement but of those with heaviest responsibility for its creation and maintenance. The distinction made clear in the Council's Constitution continues to be valid and of the utmost importance.

The conditioning clauses of the Constitution are nevertheless as important as its main assertions. '. . . in such matters as one or more of them [the member churches] shall commit to it . . . as may be specified by the constituent churches.' The means by which churches may be held to 'commit' to the Council responsibility for action or 'specify' lines of action are varied; initiatives resulting in such mandates may come from various quarters, not excluding the leadership of the Council, but at some vital point in every programme of action the administration is invariably dependent upon the authority of the churches and is answerable to them.

In the foregoing pages there have been briefly described some areas of action which have involved the raising and disbursing of considerable sums of money by the Council itself. This in turn has required substantial administrative machinery through which such action can be effected. In addition to the undertakings touched on in this chapter there is, of course, the vast enterprise of relief and service represented by the term 'Christian aid' and conducted from within the Council by its Division of Inter-Church Aid, Refugee and World Service. All this action by the Council itself has originated in and remains contingent upon the express mandate of the churches, an authority which could be withdrawn at any moment if the churches so wished. Yet even where the Council has assumed these administrative responsibilities it is worth noting certain characteristics which are always apparent in their discharge and which are related to the main emphases of the Constitution.

First, such centralized administration as the Council undertakes never represents more than a small part of the total money raised and the work done by the churches and their own agencies in any specific undertaking. In relation to any one field of concern the decentralized responsibility is far greater than that which is carried by the Council itself. Even in the large and complex undertakings of the Division of Inter-Church Aid, Refugee and World Service, while substantial funds (as in the Division's service programme) are directly administered by the Council, these are little more than token contributions towards needs for which far more is raised and given by the churches or other agencies. Further, the main money raising responsibility for Inter-Church Aid and Service to Refugees is carried not by the World Council but by national organizations such as Christian Aid in Great Britain, Church World Service in the U.S.A., Diakonische Werk in Germany, and comparable organizations in many other countries. This same principle of decentralized responsibility is even more markedly in evidence in the work of the other enterprises referred to in this chapter, namely the Theological Education Fund, the Agency for Christian Literature Development, and the Christian Medical Commission. Such financial resources as attach to these activities are applied either to strengthening existing institutions which depend on other sources for their regular maintenance, or to making possible the beginning of new ventures whose ultimate support is assured from other sources.

Secondly, all these aiding operations of the World Council are on a short-term basis. There is no possibility of the Council undertaking the permanent financial assistance even of the most praiseworthy projects. Thirdly, in the process of ascertaining needs in the making of decisions to meet them, and in the actual administration of help it is an essential policy of the Council always to work through local agencies—member churches or national Christian Councils. It is on this local responsibility that the ultimate effectiveness of all these practical operations of the Council depend.

Finally, it is a matter of pre-eminent concern to the World Council that any financial and personal assistance it can offer shall be applied where it is likely to stimulate local initiative in thought and action. Where the meeting of unmet needs appears to wait on some fresh incentive, encouragement, or assistance the Council may find itself able to offer help on terms which will have the effect of a catalyst in the local situation. John R. Mott, one of the greatest of the ecumenical pioneers in modern times, was fond of describing particular occasions, actions, and personal meetings as 'highly multiplying'. Mott was blessed with insight, abilities, and a personal dynamism which more often than not justified this description of any experience in which he was involved. What the World Council tries to exert amidst the many ramifications of its practical service is this highly multiplying influence for the sake of ends beyond itself.

Like the word 'church' the term 'ecumenical' points to a reality
which must be seen to be both universal and particular. These are
two inseparable aspects of a single whole. In so far as institutions
can embody the life of the Church or the ecumenical movement
they need to be both local and worldwide. Each is dependent on
the other and necessary to the other.

It has been said that if the World Council of Churches had not
come into existence when it did something very much like it would
soon have had to be organized. That is to say, there have been at
work in our time forces which have kindled the kind of vision and
concern, conviction and experience which have come to be associated
with the term 'ecumenical'. These forces would in any circumstances have necessitated some organized expression on an international basis. Something like a world council, whatever its internal
pattern, would have been an inevitable response to the experience
and needs of this era in history. Nevertheless, such an international
structure would have been meaningless apart from the locally
organized expressions of the same worldwide convictions and needs.
The most crucial of these local expressions are the churches, but
both the churches and the worldwide organization of which they
are the essential components have become increasingly dependent
in certain respects on councils of churches which base their membership upon particular regions, countries, or towns. These regional
and national Christian councils within a particular town or group
of parishes have multiplied greatly in recent years. They vary considerably in their composition, basis of membership, their resources,
and not least their effectiveness, but at their best they provide
growing points within the total ecumenical movement, and are important instruments for ecumenical action.

At present there are three principal regional councils with two
or three others in process of becoming so. The three well-established
ones are the East Asia Christian Conference, the All Africa Conference of Churches, and the Conference of Pacific Churches.

East Asia
The East Asia Christian Conference was formally inaugurated
in 1959 but by then it had already been in process of formation
for some years. Three principal motives lay behind its creation.

First, there was the desire of Asian Christian leaders for closer and
more regular contact with one another. Secondly, there was the
realization that the churches in any one Asian country knew all too
little of other Asian churches—a lack which needed to be remedied
for their common enrichment and for the strengthening of their
witness throughout the continent. Thirdly, it was greatly desired
that ways should be found of channelling more effectively than
hitherto the contribution of the Asian churches to the ecumenical
understanding of the faith and of the life and witness of the Church
universal. Towards the achievement of these aims there was convened at Bangkok in 1949 an exploratory conference of church
leaders from ten Asian countries. One outcome of this meeting was
the appointment, under the joint auspices of the International
Missionary Council and the World Council of Churches, of an East
Asia Secretary. An Indian Lutheran, Rajah B. Manikam, was un-
animously chosen for this post, which was described as that of an
'ambassadorial representative' who would visit the churches and
Christian councils in East Asia 'helping them to share more fully
their thought and experience with a view to strengthening the
churches in their evangelistic task in East Asia and establishing
closer contact than at present exists between the East Asian churches
and councils and the worldwide movement of the Church'. What
soon became this ambassadorial representative's dominant concern
amidst his many journeys and discussions is well illustrated in the
title of a book which he edited—*Christianity and the Asian Revolution*. The book was a powerful symposium by Asian writers and it
is still relevant to an appreciation of the position and task of the
Asian churches.

The term 'revolution' dominated the next representative gathering of East Asian Christians, which was held in Indonesia in 1957.
In fact, the meeting opened only a few days after the ending of a
state of emergency in the region. Twelve Asian countries were
represented, though an expected delegation from the Chinese
churches was prevented from attending. Apart from wrestling with
the main theme of the conference—The Common Evangelistic
Task in Revolutionary Asia—further attention was given to the
shape which a permanent regional organization might take, and
two years later the East Asia Christian Conference was formally
inaugurated at Kuala Lumpur in Malaya, with an initial membership representing forty-eight churches from fourteen countries. A
small permanent staff working with consultative groups convened
from time to time and maintaining close liaison with the World
Council of Churches as well as with the churches and Christian
councils in the region has since made this Asian organization a most

valuable instrument in the service of the churches in the region and
within the life of the World Council. The Conference carries a large
share of responsibility for the World Council's programme of inter-
church aid and service to refugees. It has sponsored the creation of
an Association of Theological Schools in South East Asia. It has
done much to promote the inter-change of personnel between the
churches and to foster their concern for the worldwide witness of
the Church. Some of its most vital work is done through *ad hoc*
groups and personal staff service, but its official assemblies have always been occasions of considerable significance for the Asian
churches themselves and for the ecumenical movement generally.
The fourth of these assemblies was held in Bangkok in 1968 and a
fifth is due in 1972.

At the 1968 meeting the subjects discussed included the role of
Asian Christians in political, economic, and international affairs,
Christianity and urban and industrial problems, Christianity in the
Asian academic world and in the Christian–Muslim encounter. 'A
divided Church in a broken world' was one of the principal themes
running through the conference and out of an appraisal of a number of schemes of church union in various parts of the world some
'guidelines to church union' were formulated. Much attention was
given to the subject of missionary service in Asian countries—a
topic which began not with the place of western missionaries but
of Asian missionaries serving in other countries than their own.
The number of such now runs into several hundreds and some are
serving farther afield than Asia, including Europe and the United
States of America. 'Every church is both a sending and a receiving
church', said the report on this subject. Steps were taken to facilitate the use of the regional conference as a clearing-house in the
placing of missionaries and the transmission of funds for their
support. On the future of western missionaries serving in Asian
countries some significant assertions were made:

The Church is a worldwide reality and should as far as possible be
manifestly seen to be so. Missionaries are an expression of the universal
nature of the Church. If the Asian churches are rightly to confess their
faith on Asian soil they need the help of Western churches in seeking to
understand the treasures of the faith they have received in the vessels
which came from the west.

We affirm that churches in Asia still require the use of western missionaries
and that churches in the west increasingly require the services of Asian
missionaries. The churches will have to reconsider far more deliberately
than they do at present how to ensure that western missionaries are fully
accepted in their fellowship and not left to find their own way. Great
openness and self-searching humility are required on both sides if there

is to be any genuine fellowship in life and witness between Asians and westerners in Asia today.

With this acceptance of a Christian imperative both to send and to receive, the conference nevertheless had to reckon with increasing restrictions imposed by governments on the entry of western missionaries into Asian countries. In face of this and also taking into account 'the maturity of Churches in Asia', it was urged that 'consideration be given to establishing a ceiling on the number of western missionaries, especially from one country, assigned to any one church in order to ensure the health and growth of the church and its own personnel'.

Perhaps one of the signs of the healthy condition of this regional conference can be seen in another sentence of the Bangkok report which reads: 'We sound a warning against a mere proliferation of committees and consultations as sometimes a substitute rather than a preparation for action.'

Africa

It was to the beating of African drums that the All Africa Conference of churches came into existence in 1963 at Kampala, Uganda. As with the East Asia Christian Conference there had been an earlier period of preparation and the decision to create the regional organization had been taken at a widely representative meeting at Ibadan, Nigeria, in 1958. In the brief period between 1958 and 1963 about twenty African nations had acquired political independence and this phenomenon, with all the turbulence and high expectation which accompanied it, inevitably coloured the thought and dominant concerns of the new All Africa organization. (It is of some interest to note that the decision to form a Christian regional conference for Africa was taken five years before the formation of the political Organization for African Unity.) The new Conference, whose membership is now drawn from over forty countries and more than thirty denominations, included Christian Councils within which a good deal of thought had been given to the special demands which this context of political aspiration and independence might make on the churches. In connexion with the World Council's series of studies in Rapid Social Change some notable contributions have been made to clarifying the meaning of 'Christian participation in nation building', and in 1965 a group of extremely able African Christian laymen published a document on 'The Christian Response to the African Revolution'. When the next full assembly of the All Africa Conference of Churches met in 1969 at Abidjan in the Ivory Coast, the secretary could say in his report that most participants had come from countries which had been independent for a few years and 'were learning from stark reality what it really means to be the Church in the situation created by the aftermath of independence'. One of the addresses at this meeting was appropriately entitled 'Fire on all horizons'. The absence of an official delegation from Nigeria was a symptom of what had been happening in the post-independence era. The absence was due to the fact that the country in which the assembly was held, the Ivory Coast, had recognized Biafra—an offence for which the Nigerian government had severed diplomatic relations. There was much plain speaking at this meeting on the abuse 'by governments and individuals' of newly acquired power and the churches were asked how, in face of oppressive policies and practices, they were fulfilling 'their appointed task' of reconciliation. . . . Do they pretend that the situations do not exist and therefore do nothing about them? If they are anxious to take the Gospel seriously what must they do to make it relevant?' These were questions addressed by Africans to Africans but they needed to be overheard by the churches in every continent.

Like the East Asia Christian Conference the African organization carries a large share of responsibility for helping to frame and implement the policies and programmes of the World Council's Division of Inter-Church Aid, Refugee and World Service. In particular it has been heavily involved in the allocation of the World Council's Emergency Fund for Africa to which the Uppsala Assembly gave a larger mandate with the promise of larger resources. Educational policy, and especially the role of churches and missions within greatly expanded and accelerated government programmes; problems of family life, particularly in the context of traditionally polygamous societies; the right theological and pastoral approach to African religious beliefs and inherited customs— these are all areas of concern and responsibility in which the All Africa Conference of Churches is daily involved. As elsewhere also the question of the meaning of Christian unity and of diversities within unity in the ordering of the Church are high on the continuing agenda of the Conference. One aspect of this universal question presses with particular insistence within Africa. This has to do with the existence and fantastically swift proliferation of 'African independent churches', whose number now runs into thousands. The Abidjan Assembly described this phenomenon as 'a movement of both schism and renewal. It is schism because of the multiplicity of divisions taking place, splitting the established churches as well as dividing the newly separated groups. Nevertheless it is renewal for it challenges the historic churches to examine their own life and open themselves to the possibility of learning from the independent churches what it means to root the Gospel in the needs of particular African communities.'[1] To foster a better understanding of this situation and to assist in determining right relationships with it the Assembly decided on the appointment to its staff of someone 'with training in theology and if possible in African sociology, with gifts of sensitivity and the ability to communicate . . . and speaking both French and English if possible'. The All Africa Conference of Churches is clearly not content with mediocre equipment in those who serve the cause for which it stands.

The Pacific

One of the few remaining British Colonies and one of the smallest in population appears on most maps as a scattering of scarcely distinguishable dots in about two million square miles of water. This is the Gilbert and Ellice Islands Colony, one of many island groups in the South Pacific. Others of these 'astonishing clusters'—as one of the early missionaries to the region described them—are more substantial in their land area and within this same region there is the extensive territory of Papua–New Guinea. In few areas of the world has the transition from the primitive to the sophisticated been as swift as here. (A little more than thirty years ago I stood by an almost naked Papuan who carried his bow and arrow while we watched the landing of an aeroplane.) In so vast and diversified an area there are of course great cultural as well as geographical and economic differences and the territories and their inhabitants are at varying stages of development and sophistication. There are communities, chiefly in Papua–New Guinea, in which the leap from stone age to nuclear age has been precipitated within two or three decades. This propulsion, with all its bewildering and tumultuous consequences, was triggered off when from 1940 onwards the Pacific became one of the critical 'theatres' of war. This cataclysm and its aftermath finally exploded the myth of an idyllic and more or less innocent South Seas where life on its sun-drenched beaches escaped the pressures and acids of modernity.

This vast area, more water than land, comes within the orbit of the Pacific Conference of Churches, another of the well-established regional expressions of the ecumenical movement. In 1959 the London Missionary Society (the pioneer mission in the area) initiated correspondence with some of the churches and with other missions in the Pacific with a view to the holding of a consultation on common problems, especially those which had arisen or become intensified since the end of war. Discussion resulted

[1] See *Engagement*, the Report of the Second Assembly of the All Africa Conference of Churches, published in Nairobi, Kenya, by the Council in 1970.

in a request for the International Missionary Council to take responsibility for convening such a gathering, and after a period of intense preparation conducted within the area itself, a conference was held at Samoa in 1961. All the main island groups, such as Fiji, Solomon Islands, Tahiti, Tonga, New Caledonia, the New Hebrides, as well as Papua–New Guinea, Australia, and New Zealand were represented. It was soon realized that the kind of needs which were bringing churches together in East Asia and Africa, especially the need to overcome isolation and to confer on common problems, were not only present in the Pacific but had been accentuated by the geography of the area and the late development of communications. It is not surprising, therefore, that what had been convened as an *ad hoc* consultation in Samoa led to a decision to form a more permanent regional organization. This was formally constituted five years later in an inaugural assembly at Lifu in 1966, with a Samoan pastor as its secretary. A second assembly was held in Fiji in 1971.

The basic concerns which have thrust themselves upon the attention of churches everywhere, inevitably appeared in the agenda of the 1966 meeting and they continue to engage the thought and energies of the churches in the Pacific: the ministry, its nature, training, and employment; the unity of the Church, especially in a region where geographical isolation has combined with denominational insularity to harden separation; the nature of a Christian society and its implications for tribal communities; the Christian conception of the family and its relation to other community patterns, especially to 'customary' marriage; and, penetrating all else, the special pressures and problems which have become universal in the aftermath of two world wars and through the spread of a worldwide technological culture. The mere existence of a regional conference, with its great assemblies occurring at five-yearly intervals, its smaller specialized consultations convened in the intervals, and its one permanent secretary who lives on pilgrimage is structurally a slender instrument through which to focus the thinking of churches scattered over so great and diversified an area. Nevertheless it is a symbol of the unity of Christ's people amidst the greatest diversities and the most formidable physical separation and within its modest resources the Conference of the Pacific Churches is proving to be a worthy servant of the servants of Christ.

The Middle East

In the Middle East there is an organization called the Near East Council of Churches. The terms '*Near* East', '*Far* East', and '*Middle* East' betray the location of those who in an earlier day devised identification labels for particular geographical and political entities. *Near* what? *Far* from whom? In the *middle* of whose maps? The Near East Council of Churches began in a day when the phrase 'east of Suez' still meant for most westerners a world beyond the familiar. Far beyond that frontier lay the East of greatest difference but in the middle distance there were territories relatively near the dominating centres of the western world. The Christian missions were not responsible for inventing the geographical terms but it was the missions of Europe and America which joined their forces to form what has become the present Near East Council of Churches. Its origins are much older than those of the Asian, African, or Pacific Councils and its initial incentive had to do with the great question of the Christian approach to the Muslim world.

In the nineteen-twenties in the judgement of some of the most scholarly Christian students of Islam, supported by missionary experience, the Muslim world was offering an unprecedented opportunity for Christian witness. 'Of the population of the Muslim world . . . we find that no less than four-fifths are now increasingly accessible to every method of missionary approach. . . . From nearly every part of the field we have reports of a responsive spirit, a new willingness to hear the Gospel message and much less antagonism than in former days.'[2] These words appear in the report of a conference of workers amongst Muslims held in Jerusalem in 1924. Incidentally, lest this optimism of fifty years ago should be thought to be part of the same over-simplifying assumptions about the demands of authentic Christian witness to Muslims, it is worth noting the report's contention that a right response to the new opportunities would require 'a change of emphasis in the life of the missionary and of the community associated with him'. A merely activist 'home of organization and good works' was an inadequate base for what was most needed, namely a profound spiritual encounter with the spirit of Islam. The 'mission house' must become 'a home of prayer, even at the cost of refusing some other opportunities for service. . . . Not only private prayer but communal worship should have a more central place in the activities of any missionary group.' Looking towards the possibility of greater cooperation between western missions to the Muslim world and the ancient Eastern churches in the region the report added:

In communion with God differences between eastern and Western mentality cease to count; common worship may be the greatest unifying force between Oriental and Western workers and may call for that sacrificial living which no amount of able organization and teaching can demand.

[2] *Letters and Papers of John R. Mott*, Vol. V, New York Association Press, 1947, pp. 332 ff.

This Jerusalem conference of 1924 had been preceded by three smaller consultations in Algeria, Egypt, and Syria, and it was followed by another in Iran. Each of these drew together representatives of missions from a cluster of surrounding countries and it was as a result of this process that the decision was taken to create a 'Christian Council for Western Asia and Northern Africa', which held its first meeting in 1927. In 1929 the name was changed to the Near East Christian Council. Initially only missionary societies and the mission boards of churches constituted the membership of the Council but at its fifth meeting in 1935 it was decided to 'prepare the way for the inclusion of any of, or all the indigenous bodies which might desire it'. Even five years later when the Armenian Evangelical Union of Syria and Lebanon and the Episcopal Church in Egypt became members, concern was expressed that the Council remained a predominantly missionary organization. If it was to become the more representative body which it sought to be something must be done, it was acknowledged, 'to foster a greater ecumenical spirit'.

The most difficult aspect of this problem arose from the position of the great and ancient Orthodox Churches of the Middle East. The Jerusalem Conference in 1924 had, in fact, been held in the Greek Church on the Mount of Olives at the invitation of the Greek Patriarch. Men delegates were housed in the Patriarch's Summer Palace and women in the Russian convent where all met for meals in the convent refectory. Such personal courtesies have not been lacking since; indeed they have greatly multiplied. But the question of more formal co-operation implying membership in a common organization has always raised difficulties in a region where most of the younger indigenous churches, whether Protestant or Anglican, are composed of converts whose traditional membership and loyalty have been rooted in Orthodoxy. From the Orthodox standpoint, therefore, these churches are the product of proselytism and schism, while the more 'evangelical' churches have tended to regard the dominant Orthodox Churches as being bastions of conservatism and intolerance. This situation has eased considerably in recent years, especially with the growth in ecumenical understanding and not least through the widespread participation of all denominations in the region in the annual Week of Prayer for Christian Unity. Further, the bringing into the open of the vexed question of proselytism through the World Council's fundamental study on Christian Witness, Proselytism, and Religious Liberty has also played an important part in the improvement in relationships.

Negotiations are in fact now proceeding which could lead to a

reconstruction of the Near East Council of Churches on a basis which
would facilitate a more completely ecumenical membership. If this
is to be realized it will be impossible to ignore another vital factor
which has become of increasing importance since the Second Vatican
Council, namely the possibility of new relationships between the
Roman Catholic Church and the other Churches in the Middle
East. For some years good relationships have existed in such areas
of concern and common action as the appalling refugee problem.
Again in the supremely important field of biblical scholarship a new
Arabic translation of the Scriptures is in hand on which, under
the aegis of the United Bible Societies, Roman Catholic, Orthodox,
and Protestant scholars are engaged. It is out of such undertakings
as these and the confidence and growth in mutual understanding
which they engender that the way becomes clearer towards the
development of right relationships on a more formal basis. Meantime, the present Near East Council of Churches has not forgotten
the original incentive which prompted the 1924 venture in co-
operation. Amidst its many more recent demands and problems it
has continued to provide the setting in which some of the most
searching and fruitful of the new 'dialogue' encounters with Islam
have been initiated.

Latin America

In an era when such words as revolution and violence, upheaval,
turbulence and turmoil can be applied to almost any part of the
world, the great sub-continent of Latin America continues to add its
characteristic explosiveness to these terms and to the situations
they describe. The addition applies to something more than negative
protest and revolt. It reflects a certain dynamism of character, an
intense and exuberant liveliness, a tempo in thought, speech, and
action to be marked *presto* rather than *andante*. It is in keeping
with this ethos that the most fast-growing religious movement in
most of the Latin American Republics is Pentecostalism.

Historically Latin America has for centuries been the home of a
dominant Roman Catholicism closely linked in many instances
with the most powerful economic strongholds and traditional centres
of power. Over against this predominance of Rome there has
emerged an active, militant Protestantism much of which is the outcome of missions, chiefly from North America, which on conservative theological grounds are either hostile to or lack sympathy with
an ecumenism which is not content to write off Rome as anti-Christ.
During a tour of some Latin American countries in 1962 I paid an
unheralded call on an educational missionary of whose work I had
heard good reports. When I had introduced myself this brother in

Christ said, 'If you come from the World Council of Churches I don't want to see you. I don't want anyone from the World Council to look at my school and then say that I've welcomed him.' I assured my resisting host that I could survive without seeing his school but as a Christian minister I was interested to know why a fellow minister felt as he did about the World Council. After a long discussion on the Bible, the faith, and the Church my now more amiable friend gave me tea and asked me to look around the school. I said I would rather not embarrass him and sully the school's reputation by a visit from the World Council of Churches, to which he replied 'Then come and look at it as a friend.' This incident reflects something that is more than incidental to the Christian enterprise in Latin America. There is this paradox of a capacity for goodwill between individuals committed to the cause of Christ but prevented from giving a natural expression to the goodwill by presuppositions and prejudices, fears and false images, as well as doctrinal rigidities that arise almost insuperable barriers. The tragedy is that this so often gathers around such a goodwill word as 'evangelical'. This attitude to the ecumenical movement does not represent the whole of the non-Roman religious forces in Latin America but it is widespread and persistent, often carrying with it grievous consequences.

Pentecostalism, while representing in some of its manifestations a theological conservatism, cannot simply be identified with the other expressions of conservative evangelicalism. Its basic convictions, its emphasis on experience more than on doctrine, and its multiform character make it far from rigid in organization or relationships. Beginning as a revival movement capable of finding expression within any of the existing church structures and originally disclaiming the idea of becoming a separate denomination it has for the most part sat lightly to structural uniformity and 'order'. Its own progress has compelled it, as with all such movements, to come to terms with the necessity for institutional forms—church buildings, recognized ministries, and even a world organization called the World Pentecostal Fellowship. At the moment these necessities are forcing upon it many of the problems, with their consequent tensions, familiar in all revival movements. Nevertheless, there are infinite variations within the many institutional forms of Pentecostalism. In some countries some Pentecostal churches have found it fairly easy to become members of national Christian councils, while others continue to be indifferent to, or opposed to, any such commitments. It was a significant moment when, at the New Delhi Assembly of the World Council two Pentecostal Churches in Chile became members of the Council. Only one other Pentecostal Church has

since joined though there are a number of points at which co-operation is being developed.

In contrast to the non-cooperative attitude of the more conserva-
evangelical groups the missions of those churches in North America
and Europe which at an early date were involved in the ecumenical
movement soon recognized the need to develop formal instruments
of co-operation. As far back as 1913 a meeting convened by what
was then the Foreign Missions Conference of North America (the
American equivalent of the Conference of British Missionary
Societies) resolved to create a permanent Committee on Co-operation
in Latin America. This decision led to a powerful gathering at
Panama in 1916 when over 300 delegates, about half of whom were
Latin American 'nationals', gave evidence of an eager desire for
greater co-operation in every aspect of the work of churches and
missions. There followed a series of smaller conferences in eight
different countries—Argentina, Brazil, Chile, Peru, Colombia,
Cuba, and Puerto Rica—one consequence of which was the creation
of a number of local Christian councils or committees on co-operation. Most of these eventually became constituent members of the
International Missionary Council which throughout its history enjoyed the vigorous participation of some extremely able Latin
American delegations.

Significant as were these steps, the range of co-operation which
they represented remained limited by the fact that the more conservative evangelicals and most of the Pentecostalists kept aloof
from the movement. Further, there was little or no contact between
these national councils and the Orthodox Churches where they
existed within the same area. Again, in the circumstances of the
time there was little possibility of any fraternal dealings with the
Roman Catholic Church. In the years immediately following the
second world war some new factors began to affect the situation.
First there were the World Council of Churches activities in Latin
America. In connexion with the programme of the Division of
Inter-Church Aid, Refugee and World Service these included not
only assistance to indigenous churches but the meeting of the needs
of immigrants by resettlement programmes in which some Latin
American countries played a large role as receiving countries.
Secondly there was the impact on Latin America of the World
Council's studies in Rapid Social Change and the growing involvement of many Latin American Protestants in the more radical movements of social reform. Thirdly, after the second Vatican Council
some of the most remarkable changes in Roman Catholic–Protestant
relationships began to be experienced in Latin America, contrary to
the widely held assumption that Roman Catholicism in the continent

would be least amenable to change and that the evangelical forces would be suspicious of any friendly overtures from such a quarter. All these influences began to produce new alignments in church as well as personal relationships, resulting in very multiform patterns of co-operation.

Amid such diversity, displayed over so wide an area and in situations characterized by constant change, attempts to create a single regional structure have always been beset by difficulties. From time to time the more conservative evangelicals have organized national evangelical conferences which have drawn their membership from many Latin American countries and have included at least some participants who see no contradiction between the terms 'evangelical' and 'ecumenical'. In connexion with the World Council of Churches activities already mentioned, there have been a number of *ad hoc* meetings with a wide range of representation, and a Commission on Education in which the World Council of Christian Education has played a considerable part aims at serving the whole of Latin America. Further, in 1964 there was appointed a Provisory Committee for Evangelical Unity through which it was hoped that churches and missions which were equally concerned about evangelical and ecumenical progress might establish a more fully representative and permanent regional council. This, however, is an aim which has still to be accomplished. Whatever the further course of such endeavours one thing is indubitable. With its extraordinary diversity of religious institutions, their potency and volatility and their relation to the social and cultural ferment of the continent, Latin America is likely to be the source of some extremely significant and exciting contributions to ecumenical thought and action in the years ahead.

Europe
It is obvious that all these regional councils are attempting an almost impossible task in trying to comprehend in one overall pattern enormous differences, geographical, cultural, linguistic as well as ecclesiastical. In Europe the task is being undertaken in a situation made more complex by the acute political differences between Western and Eastern Europe. The first meeting of the churches from both parts of Europe was held in Nyborg, Denmark, in 1959. Since then five other meetings have been convened and at the third of these, in 1964, the Constitution of a regional council to be known as the Conference of European Churches was adopted. Some of the best work of this Conference has been done through fairly small working parties and commissions meeting between the larger assemblies. These have bridged in their membership, if not in their

agreements, the differing standpoints of Eastern and Western European churchmen. Between the fifth and sixth assemblies of this Conference of European Churches (1968 to 1971) working groups of this character discussed together such themes as the Church's Ministry to Society and Ecclesiological Questions in Modern European Society. It is not surprising that on such themes as these the groups have found it easier to reach unanimity in the formulation of questions than in the discovery of answers. Nevertheless it is some evidence of the reality and the potentialities of the ecumenical movement that churches separated by such frontiers as at present divide Europe are committed to one another in this continuing quest. At the 1971 assembly in Nyborg, which was attended by delegates from more than a hundred churches, all countries in Europe were represented with the single exception of Albania.

National Councils

The member units of the World Council of Churches are churches, not regional or national councils of churches, but the links between these councils, all of which are independent, autonomous bodies and the World Council itself are for practical purposes very close. A national council may, with the approval of the World Council's Central Committee, become formally related to the Council as an Associate Council. With this status it may be invited to send a non-voting representative to World Council Assemblies and to meetings of the Central Committee. The constitutional requirement for this status is that the national council 'knowing the Basis upon which the World Council of Churches is founded expresses its desire to co-operate with the World Council toward the achievement of one or more of the functions and purposes of the Council'. At present there are twenty-five of these Associate Councils. In addition to these the World Council has regular working relationships with about another sixty national councils some of which are specially related to the Commission on World Mission and Evangelism. All these vary greatly in size and resources, in the range of their membership, and the nature of their activities.

The National Council of the Churches of Christ in the U.S.A. incorporates in its large and complex structure a number of older national organizations concerned with Christian unity, home and foreign missions, Christian education, Christian social service, international affairs, and the role of women in the churches' life and witness. The Council's budget and staff exceed that of the World Council itself and it maintains an extensive service to the churches and on their behalf in almost every aspect of their witness. The

Canadian and British Councils of Churches, with those in the Netherlands, Germany, and a number of countries in Asia and Africa are well established with whole-time staffs and a considerable range of activity. Some other national councils are dependent on part-time staff service and are correspondingly more limited in their operations. In the long run perhaps the most important feature of all of these structures, whatever their size and administrative strength, is that they provide not only a regular forum for discussion between their member churches but some measure of common action. They offer, and in many cases prove to be, more than casual opportunities for better understanding and for furthering the mission and unity of the Church.

While regional councils fulfil a particular function across national boundaries, and national councils facilitate co-operation within a particular country, one of the most critical growing points (or stagnation points) in the ecumenical movement lies within the smaller area of local councils organized within single cities and towns. These have multiplied enormously in recent years. In America there are close on a thousand of them. In Britain the number is around 700. Again the variations are infinite. Many do in fact constitute some of the most vital centres not only of united witness but of growth in a common understanding of the Church's nature and mission, and in progress towards the achievement of unity and greater obedience in mission. Others are only tentatively moving towards equipping themselves for these tasks. Some others, again, are too weak or too unsure about their aim or too little convinced of their own necessity to be of any great significance at the moment.

At all these 'levels'—regional, national and local—one of the most interesting, challenging, and potentially fruitful developments during the last few years has been an outcome of that new climate in relations between the Roman Catholic Church and other churches which is having its effect upon every aspect of the ecumenical movement. In the regional councils there is at least Roman Catholic 'observer' participation, with varying degrees of co-operation in study and in particular aspects of the churches' service to the world. In the Caribbean it is expected that in 1972 arrangements now well advanced will result in the establishment of a regional council which will begin with the full membership of Anglican, Methodist, Moravian, Presbyterian, and Roman Catholic Churches. Of the eighty national councils with which the World Council has regular working contacts ten have full Roman Catholic membership while many others enjoy at least fraternal or observer participation. This trend appears to be accelerating still more markedly at the level of local councils. (In Britain it is reckoned that about 73 per cent of the local councils now include some form of Roman Catholic participation.)

As with all other aspects of the ecumenical movement in its organizational expression, this large, widespread, and greatly diversified 'conciliar' development is subject to many questions and not a few criticisms. To begin with there is the simple fact that the maintenance of all these agencies costs money. More seriously than this it costs time. It draws on the energies of people who, if the councils are to be truly representative, usually hold very demanding positions of responsibility in their churches and have little time to spare. At this point the councils in the less economically favoured areas are specially vulnerable. The cost of the secretarial service of the regional councils in East Asia and Africa is largely borne by the World Council of Churches or one of its agencies, and the majority of the national councils in these regions are also to a large extent financially dependent on assistance from the World Council, the mission boards of America and Europe, or on other international agencies which desire to channel their help to the churches through a central co-ordinating body. Basically this is only one aspect of the sharing of resources between the churches of the world, but it can result in some uneasiness, first, because there is felt to be a connexion between financial independence and the ability of a council truly to reflect the ethos of the area which it primarily serves; secondly, because in any time of financial stringency it is difficult for many of the contributing churches even in this age of growing ecumenical awareness, not to regard these councils as 'outside bodies' instead of seeing them as necessary expressions of the churches' interdependence.

Again, while a regional, national or local council is at all times dependent on its member units, is responsible to them and exists to serve them, in the nature of the case it develops an identity of its own and becomes something more than the mechanical recording or transmitting instrument of the churches. Even when it undertakes tasks which could not be attempted or handled adequately by the churches in separation and is therefore functioning strictly on behalf of its members, its resulting actions are seldom likely to be along lines which commend themselves to all the members of all the churches. This is notoriously true of situations in which a council feels itself called upon to make pronouncements in its own name and on behalf of its member churches, or when it initiates studies and seeks to provide the churches with material for discussion on controversial issues such as race, sex, labour conditions, national policies, or international affairs. 'The council isn't speaking for us', some churches and church members will protest. 'It is going beyond its mandate.' 'Those people up there don't know what they're talking about.' 'The council is interfering in politics.' Thus the next move in a synod or other church session will be a proposal to reduce the church's subscription to the council or to agitate for withdrawal of membership. So the council becomes regarded as a tiresome extra, if not a dangerous nuisance, which the churches could better dispense with in order to get on with their own job. This of course is only delaying such fundamental questions as: What is any church's 'own' job? and, where in fact is the Church amidst its myriad manifestations and forms? These are the questions which constitute the heart of *the* ecumenical question. The real issue is not whether we can avoid the questions or legitimately dismiss them as irrelevant, but whether organizations whose very existence and activity sharpen them in particular contexts—regional, national or local—are doing so in a sufficiently responsible and competent manner and are providing ways and means through which the churches in costly and demanding fellowship can 'ask their way to Zion with their faces thitherward'. Can a Christian council within its particular situation, with its membership, its resources, competence, and dedication, play a worthy part, though of necessity a transitional one, in assisting all the churches to be or to become the Church? It will be necessary to return to this question and apply it to the World Council of Churches itself in the next chapter.

The World Council of Churches is not what it was. Something would be wrong if it were. The scale and complexity of its present tasks, its share of the financial anxieties from which no institutions can be exempt, and some inevitable uncertainties about its future course may induce some of its older friends to sigh for an earlier day when the future seemed less clouded and the present simpler to cope with. For these, nostalgia may tempt to the conclusion that the glory has departed. Those were the days! A younger generation may find— as many of its representatives are undoubtedly finding—that organizations and causes outside the Church speak with greater immediacy and relevance to their Christian concern for social action and world service than do any of the churches' organizations and programmes. These people may include the World Council in their abandonment of the churches. Church leaders and administrators, increasingly burdened by their immediate local and institutional responsibilities, may find themselves driven to readjust priorities and the use of time and resources with consequences which weaken their conviction of the relative importance of ecumenical organizations. Support for the World Council, as well as for national councils of churches and other agencies, may thus be reduced, not only financially but in the attention given to them and the calibre of the service offered to them. Again, actions and utterances by the World Council itself in regard to matters inherently controversial—as in the aid given to liberation movements in South Africa and to American draft resisters in Canada—may provoke withdrawal of support as well as affect (for some adversely) the public image and prestige of the Council.

The World Council is experiencing all these reactions at the present time and there are elements in them all which have to be taken seriously.

Nostalgia is never a safe guide to reality, but history matters and even within the relatively short history of the World Council of Churches it can be a salutary exercise occasionally to examine subsequent developments in the light of original aims. Impatience of youth should never be taken lightly, especially when it is provoked by contemporary injustices and wrongs. As Asquith once said, 'Youth would be an ideal state if only it came a little later in life.' Unfortunately, by the time maturity has acquired the power to act with responsible zeal the weight of responsibility tends to check zeal. Organizations which evoke youth's enthusiasm and service in worthy causes should be regarded as allies, not rivals, in the Church's search for an authentic Christian pattern of society. No one who was present at the Uppsala Assembly of the World Council and has followed the Council's actions since, can charge it with overlooking this truth. The preoccupation of church leaders and officials with the immediate local problems of the institutions they serve and their jealous regard for priorities in dealing with resources of which they are stewards can result in the wrong sort of parochialism, vision, and action; it can engender a prudence which kills passion. But it can also indicate a far-reaching recognition of the fact that the universal depends on the particular, the worldwide on the local. It is for the World Council to deal understandingly with this attitude, not in the rivalry of an either/or in priorities but with the challenge of a both/and convincingly expressed in thought and action.

Critical surveys of the World Council's way of doing things and its choice of what it does have been made on several occasions in its brief history. At the Second Assembly in 1954 a considerable reshaping of the Council's administrative structure and programmes took place in the light of one of these surveys. Between the Second Assembly and the Third in 1961, the process of integrating in the Council the work of the former International Missionary Council compelled some radical rethinking of the meaning of the Church's mission and the role of a World Council in its fulfilment. The Fourth Assembly in 1968 was so little disposed to let the Council settle into a fixed pattern of operations that it instructed the Central Committee to provide for a further reappraisal of structure and programme within two years. In making this decision the Assembly accepted a proposed remit to a new Structure Committee in terms which included the following.

After twenty years of life together the member churches need to review their understanding of the significance of the World Council of Churches and the meaning of their membership in it. They need to consider what it means for the World Council as an expression of the common life of the churches that it has moved away from the limitations of the North Atlantic that gave it birth towards the third world; that the Orthodox Churches play a decisively larger role in its life; and that after Vatican II it is in a steadily ramifying partnership with the Roman Catholic and other non-member churches.

They need to consider what are the specific ways in which the World Council functions; how its life can be renewed from fresh springs of life in the churches and in the world; how the influence of official leaders of the churches (who are mostly clerical) can best be balanced with men and women, especially younger men and women, whose primary field of Christian service is in the world; and what is the specific role of the staff of the World Council of Churches and what kinds of person should be invited to its service.

They need to assess with discriminating sensitivity fundamental Christian impulses of world mission, of faith and order, of life and work, of Christian service to men in need, and of concern for international affairs which have been the concern of the Council from the beginning; to take into careful account the danger that 'new occasions teach new duties' and that time may have made 'ancient good uncouth'; and for this reason (even more than because it is unlikely that the World Council of Churches will ever have sufficient resources to enable it to undertake all that it would wish to undertake) to consider how the World Council of Churches can be both faithful and flexible in its response to the calling of God.

The new Structure Committee first submitted a draft of its proposals to a specially convened 'Reacting and Advisory Group'. This secured the critical attention of a fairly representative sample of the Council's wide constituency. After further scrutiny by the Executive Committee, the report was considered by the Central Committee, which adopted it with a few amendments. Some parts of the report, involving amendments to the Constitution, can only be finally ratified at the next Assembly in 1975, but in the main its practical recommendations can be put into effect under the authority accorded to the Central Committee by the Uppsala Assembly.

A characteristic feature of the report is indicated in its final paragraph:

The work of restructuring is not completed, nor ever will be, for the World Council of Churches is a dynamic and ever-changing body. In constant obedience to God it will always be ready to make such changes in its structure as will enable it to meet most effectively the deepest needs of mankind.

As the report also says 'Form follows function.' 'There is no one right structure', it adds. 'There is no theology of structure. Decisions must therefore be pragmatic . . .' In the appendix to this volume the result of the structural changes now being carried out can be seen in a diagram and in the quotations from new statements of function which the Central Committee has approved. Responsibilities hitherto carried within a number of divisions and departments are now being grouped within three major Programme Units—Faith and Witness, Justice and Service, Education and Communication. The first of these gives explicit recognition to the interdependence of faith and order questions and the world mission of the Church. While this interdependence has long been recognized, its general acceptance implies very different assumptions from those which mainly prevailed, for example, at a time of the World Missionary Conference in 1910 when faith and order questions were excluded from the agenda of the meeting on the ground that they were primarily the concern of the churches, not the missions. For many years the work of the former International Missionary Council and the functions of its affiliated national councils was based on this dichotomy between Church and Mission. What has long been more clearly recognized and accepted concerning the necessary identity of these categories and which found expression in 1961 in the integration of the International Missionary Council and the World Council of Churches is now further emphasized in the new structure of the World Council. Perhaps more challengingly, the inclusion of the work formerly carried on in the Department of Church and Society (as part of the old Study Division) is acknowledged to be equally relevant to a proper understanding of the ordering of the Church and the fulfilment of its mission. A good statement of the rationale of this new Unit appears in the Structure Committee report:

The Faith and Order movement has been led to see that it can fulfil its historic task of achieving the unity of the Church only by relating it to the challenges which the churches have to face in modern society. The Division of World Mission and Evangelism has been emphasizing joint action for mission and the understanding of salvation for the life of man on six continents. Church and Society has been obliged to give more attention to the fundamental theological and ecclesiological problems posed by Christian witness in society. The dialogue with men of other faiths and ideologies, though primarily the concern of the Division of World Mission and Evangelism has become an integral part of the programme of Faith and Order and Church and Society. These concerns have become more and more interconnected and it is appropriate that they be placed in fruitful tension with each other in the interest of forwarding an authentic ecumenical understanding of the faith of the Church in our world.

The title of the second Programme Unit, Justice and Service, underlies the fact that the great relief and rehabilitation undertakings of the churches are not a form of philanthropy or first aid which can be practised without regard to national policies, international relationships, the racial question or the economic needs of the underdeveloped countries. These are but differing aspects of a single task. The third of the Programme Units, Education and Communication, now incorporates in the functions and administration of the Council a wholly new attempt (following the integration of the former

World Council of Christian Education with the World Council of Churches) to deal ecumenically with the fundamental question of the meaning of education in the light of the Christian understanding of man and his destiny.

New structures will not in themselves accomplish more than those which they replace or guarantee the achievement of newly-formulated aims. Appropriate structures can, however, facilitate progress granted the right persons, the right relationships, and the necessary resources to operate the machinery. It is with this recognition that the Council is now proceeding to implement its new decisions. In the process there is clear awareness of the fact that at this stage in the ecumenical movement and in the life of the World Council itself, the new occasions which are teaching new duties reflect greater changes in the world at large than can be measured by any immediate administrative adjustments in institutions. Speaking of 'the current crises in the Christian faith and in the life of the Church', the Structure Committee's report says:

This is an era of particularly great spiritual change. The ecumenical movement and the world Council feel its repercussions in several ways: some churches undergo great internal conflicts and polarization on theological and ethical issues; the changes taking place within the Roman Catholic Church are of great importance to all Christians; groups, like some of the conservative evangelicals, become more ecumenically co-operative; a dynamic, unofficial, and anti-establishment ecumenism challenges 'official ecumenism' which it finds often restrictive and irrelevant. Restructuring must take into account the present new fluidity in the ecclesiastical situation and the challenge of new spiritual and secular movements which have altered dramatically the posture of the Church in modern society.

Amidst its manifold details and modes of expression the ecumenical movement is concerned with two fundamental relationships. First, the relation of separated churches to one another in the light of what is meant by 'The Church'. Secondly, the relation of the Church and all its parts to the world. The first of these involves the perennial questions which come within the term Faith and Order, all of which turn ultimately on the basic issue of 'What is the Church?' The second of these fundamental relationships turns on the question 'What is the Church's mission to the world and in the world, and how can it best be accomplished?'

In regard to the first of these two over-arching concerns, the most significant development in this past decade of change lies in the new role now being assumed by the Roman Catholic Church. It may be an over-simplification to say that prior to Vatican Council II there was a danger of two rival ecumenical movements appearing, despite the fact that to conceive a plurality of such movements would be contrary to the essential meaning of the word 'ecumenical'. Nevertheless, as an earlier chapter in this volume has recalled, such contacts as the World Council enjoyed with individual Roman Catholic ecumenists prior to 1961 was against a background not merely of the Roman Catholic Church's official aloofness from the Council, but of its virtual repudiation of what the World Council stood for ecumenically. It was a far cry from this to the promulgation of the Vatican Council's *Decree on Ecumenism*, of which a distinguished Jesuit has written:

Many sentences and sections of Vatican II Decrees are remarkable for the fact that they are there at all. It can truly be said that the whole Decree on Ecumenism is remarkable for that fact. In this Decree the focus is more on a 'pilgrim' Church moving toward Christ than on a movement of 'return' to the Roman Catholic Church. In this Decree the Council goes beyond the assertion that the Catholic Church is the true Church to assert that Jesus, in his Spirit, is at work in the Churches and Communities beyond the visible borders of the Catholic Church; the Council asserts that believers in Christ who are baptised are truly reborn and truly our brothers and that God uses their worship to sanctify and save them.[1]

Dr. Oscar Cullman, a Protestant scholar whose contributions to contemporary theological studies and debates are appreciated as widely by Roman Catholics as by Protestants, spoke for his fellow observers at the Vatican Council when, in commenting on this Decree on Ecumenism, he said: 'This is more than the opening of a door; new ground has been broken.'

The Decree includes a description of the ecumenical movement which might well have been a statement of the World Council of Churches. It reads:

The 'ecumenical movement' means those activities and enterprises which, according to various needs of the Church and opportune occasions, are started and organized for the fostering of unity among Christians. These are: first, every effort to eliminate words, judgements, and actions which do not respond to the conditions of separated brethren with truth and fairness and so make mutual relations between them more difficult; then, 'dialogue' between competent experts from different Churches and Communities. In their meetings which are organized in a religious spirit each explains the teachings of his Communion in greater depth and brings out clearly its distinctive features. Through such dialogue everyone gains a

[1] Walter M. Abbott, S.J., in *The Documents of Vatican II* edited by Walter M. Abbott, London, Geoffrey Chapman, 1967.

truer knowledge and more just appreciation of the teaching and religious life of both communions. In addition these communions cooperate more closely in whatever projects a Christian conscience demands for the common good. They also come together for common prayer where this is permitted. Finally all are led to examine their own faithfulness to Christ's will for the Church and, wherever necessary, undertake with vigour the task of renewal and reform.

The World Council would have wanted to make it explicit that 'the common good' includes pre-eminently the need of the world for the Gospel and that therefore, as in its own stated functions, the World Council sees the fostering of unity as inseparable from the mission of the Church. But the whole proceedings of the Vatican Council, the content of the other decrees, especially the Decree on the Church's Missionary Activity, and the nature of the co-operation which has since developed between the World Council and the Roman Catholic Church, leave little doubt about a consensus of agreement on the most central aims of the ecumenical movement. Of course, fundamental differences remain. The breaking of new ground in the Decree on Ecumenism still leaves some old ground undisturbed and on it there stand monumental edifices with something like 'No entry' signs addressed to separated brethren. But even here there is more emphasis on the brethren than on their separation, with more than a hint that Rome will continue to suffer from its own state of separation until it has itself undergone that process of renewal which the ecumenical movement is demanding from all the churches.

It is in this radically new situation that co-operation between the World Council of Churches and the Roman Catholic Church has moved so rapidly within the last few years. In addition to constant observer participation in World Council meetings, large and small, there have been the many developments which have been touched upon in preceding chapters in this volume: the strong participation of Roman Catholics in the preparatory work for the World Conference on Church and Society in 1966 and in the conference itself; the subsequent establishment of a joint secretariat of the Pontifical Commission for Justice and Peace and the World Council of Churches, and the creation of what is now a Standing Committee on Society, Development, and Peace; the growing collaboration between the Laity Department of the World Council and the Congresses of the Lay Apostolate; successive consultations between the Division of World Mission and Evangelism and the Roman Catholic Congregation for the Evangelization of Peoples, and growth in practical collaboration between the Division of Inter-Church Aid. Refugee and World Service and Caritas Internationalis. In addition to such steps as these there is now the full membership of the Roman Catholic Church in the World Council's Commission on Faith and Order and the very significant fact that twice a year there is the opportunity for the review of these developing relationships and the consideration of their long-range implications by means of the Joint Working Group, which represents the Vatican and the World Council.

All this constitutes a process which seems more likely to accelerate than to be halted in the years ahead. When these steps are seen in conjunction with the enormous increase in local collaboration between member churches of the World Council and the Roman Catholic Church (as illustrated, for example, in a preceding chapter on local councils of churches), it becomes still more clear that the World Council and the Roman Catholic Church are now living in the context of an ecumenical movement which, with all its variations, is manifestly one movement, raising comparable questions for both, stimulating and enriching and disturbing both alike. This has one important consequence, among many others, which cannot be evaded. It becomes increasingly imperative, for pragmatic as well as theological reasons, to ask 'Where is this leading?' Can co-operation go on *ad infinitum*, growing in depth and fruitfulness but never going beyond co-operation into unity? Already this question confronts the existing member churches of the World Council in their relationship to one another. It becomes increasingly inescapable in their attitude to the Roman Catholic Church. In the dealings of its member churches with Rome the World Council cannot, and would not attempt to influence the course which any church might take. The statement at the Fourth Assembly on this reiterates the constitutional position of the Council:

The World Council of Churches has no authority to speak and act in place of its member churches. The dialogue and the collaboration with the Roman Catholic Church carried out by the Joint Working Group does not abrogate any aspect of the authority of the member churches. They alone are responsible for decisions concerning church relations.

Yet the question 'Where is this leading?', which arises insistently as co-operation proceeds, inevitably impinges on the World Council itself. The Council is more than a series of *ad hoc* ventures in co-operation between divided churches. It is not a loose and in-determinate agency to facilitate a certain amount of common action and useful discussion. It is a fellowship of churches with an explicit basis on which its members 'stay together' and work together for the fulfilment of their common calling. While still divided, the member churches are deeply committed to one another in pursuit

of a common end, with all the costliness as well as the encouragement which such a covenant relationship involves. Good relationships with churches which do not fully commit themselves to this
are imperative for the deepest reasons, and are manifestly fruitful;
but unless the kind of commitment which membership in the Council implies is meaningless and might as well be dispensed with,
collaboration with the Roman Catholic Church, indefinitely prolonged and leading to no new form of commitment, may prove
frustrating and, to some extent, disillusioning. What form such new
commitment might take is obviously bound up with the question of
possible membership of the Roman Catholic Church in the World
Council. As already noted, this is *sub judice* and it is fully recognized
that a decision cannot be hurried. It is further understood within
the World Council that Roman Catholic acceptance of membership
would create a vastly new situation for the Council itself, with consequent changes that would be far-reaching.

Meantime, two areas in which discussion is now proceeding are
of special relevance to this. The first is an on-going study, under
the aegis of a Joint Theological Commission, of the crucial subject
of 'Apostolicity and Authority'. These terms go to the heart of the
theological differences between the churches and any fundamental
progress towards unity turns on the resolution of these differences.
The work of the Joint Commission is, of course, only one illustration
of the attention now being given to these issues in contemporary
studies and 'dialogues', but it is significant that they are now being
approached on this joint Roman Catholic–World Council basis.

The second area of discussion is in relation to the possibility of
there emerging what the Fourth Assembly of the World Council
called 'a genuinely universal council which may once more speak
for all Christians'. The mere mooting of this possibility has, as might
be expected, precipitated what promises to be a long and involved
process of debate. What would be the nature of such a council? If
it is to mark an advance on the present understanding of the word
'council' as represented by the World Council of Churches it would
presumably imply that the participants in such an event would already be enjoying a degree of communion with one another which
makes eucharistic fellowship possible. Can this be envisaged apart
from greater progress in unity between the churches as they now are?
These and kindred questions will demand deep and prolonged
attention within the churches and between them. Whatever the
outcome of this particular proposal—as yet a very tentative one—
its importance lies in a widespread awareness that the ecumenical
movement must either move or peter out, and that within this
movement the World Council of churches is always, like its mem-

ber churches, in process of formation, or rather, of reformation. The *status quo* cannot endure indefinitely. At this point it is advisable to take to heart a disturbing word spoken by Dr. Lukas Vischer at the Canterbury meeting of the World Council's Central Committee in 1969:

Whoever speaks of a goal in the future comes up against the difficulty that the sceptical audience starts its thinking from the present state of the churches. The imagination, even the imagination of faith, is usually limited to extending the lines of the present into the future with only slight modifications. But clearly the churches would have to undergo profound changes if the goal of the movement should ever be attained. Now the term 'change' leads to a consideration which is of increasing importance. . . . The question is not whether the churches are prepared to initiate certain changes in their life. Whether they wish it or not, whether they are conscious of it or not, they are in fact involved in a process of change. The question is only whether they succeed in *being the Church* in this change. Change does not necessarily contradict the nature of the Church and the accelerated change which the churches are caught in today is therefore not necessarily to be considered as an enemy but perhaps rather as a healthy reminder. Whatever may be said, in any case the churches will increasingly have to accustom themselves to the fact that they are a fellowship for which change is not an exceptional event but a fellowship which is involved in constant change. Their attention will increasingly have to focus on the next step into the future. It may even be that this capacity must be regarded as an essential quality of the Church; the freedom to establish fellowship in Christ under ever new circumstances.

For all the churches, in their relationship to one another within the one fellowship of the Spirit which is given and sustained by the one Lord, the ecumenical movement is a reminder that they are still on pilgrimage and the end is not yet.

The second of the fundamental relationships with which the ecumenical movement is concerned is the relation of the Church and all its parts to the world. Here again the keynote today is *change*, and the tempo of the change is fast. Writing in 1969 on 'Dynamic Factors in the Ecumenical Situation', Dr. Visser 't Hooft put first 'the resumption of the dialogue with the world'. The word 'resumption' was necessary, said Visser 't Hooft because 'for a long time the churches had either been ignorant of the world or else had condemned it'.[2] Like all historical generalizations, this judgement can be qualified by exceptions, but there is no doubt whatever that the main shift of emphasis in the Uppsala Assembly of the World Council, the role played in determining this shift by

[2] *The Ecumenical Review*, Vol. 21, no. 4, October 1969.

the Geneva Conference on Church and Society in 1966, and such
Roman Catholic statements as the 'Pastoral Constitution on the
Church in the Modern World' mark a major turning-point in the
acknowledgement of the churches' necessary involvement in the
world. Previous chapters have illustrated some of the consequences
of this in the policies and programmes of the World Council of
Churches, especially those in which there is increasing co-operation
not only with the Roman Catholic and other non-member churches
but with a multiplicity of governmental and other 'secular' agencies.
The Programme to Combat Racism, the Commission on the
Churches' Participation in Development, the expanding programme
of the Committee on Society, Development and Peace, the Ecumenical Enquiry on the Future of Man and Society, the study of Non-
violent Methods of Achieving Social Change, the continuing work
of the Commission of the Churches on International Affairs in the
fields of human rights and disarmament and—not least—the fact
that the theme of the latest meeting of the Faith and Order Commission is 'The Unity of the Church and the Unity of Mankind'.
all these once again bear witness to the fact that the word 'ecumenical' is a very worldly word, as well as one with ecclesiastical
implications.

To some people this trend appears to be no more than a later
edition of the 'social gospel' of an earlier day, an interpretation of
Christianity and a programme for an activist church which events
and deeper reflection eventually discredited. This is too facile a
discounting of the present involvement of the ecumenical movement in the very temporal and material aspects of man's life in this
world. This involvement is bound up with a truer recovery of the
meaning of the prophetic tradition, the implications of the incarnation and the consequences of Christ's redeeming work for man-in-
society no less than for man in his solitariness. This is not merely a
swing of the pendulum which will soon, in the nature of things, go
into reverse. Reference has already been made in this book to the
tension at Uppsala between the horizontal and the vertical. It is true
that there are those within the churches who still see this issue as an
either/or and signs of this were not absent from the Uppsala
Assembly. This was one reason why one of the disappointments of
the Assembly was the inability of the section on 'Renewal in
Mission' to restate the essential nature of the Church's mission to
the world, its abiding character, as well as its new dimensions and
its contemporary expression. Perhaps it was a mistake to sectionalize
the study of mission and not recognize that it involved everything
with which the Assembly was concerned, from Faith and Order to
Rapid Social Change. Yet at the heart of the unresolved tensions

at Uppsala—and this has become more in evidence in the short time that has passed since the last Assembly—there was a widely shared determination to resist any either/or resolution of the dilemma. What was being sought, and is still being pursued, is a deeper apprehension of what is implied by the 'point of intersection' between the vertical and the horizontal. At this point no aspect of human need is irrelevant to the Gospel; it goes into all the world and into every aspect of the life of man in this world. But it does so at a point where the sin of man involves the intersecting Cross and where the mystery of death, violent and premature, exposed the most awful dimension of human existence. Because of the nature of that intersecting Cross and all for which it stands, the Church has a word to say to human need in its totality and to the world in all its splendours and failures, which is uniquely the saving Word. Only as the churches, in their continued growth together, their travail together and their involvement in the world, learn more fully what it means to live, to think, to witness and to serve from this point of intersection will the full purpose of the ecumenical movement be realized.

8 Epilogue

The Local Church and the Ecumenical Movement
In all Christian communions today there is in evidence a recovery of the significance of the local church. It is in a particular congregation or parish that the Church catholic is to be seen. It is manifest in the worship and fellowship of a company of people living within range of one another, growing in understanding of the faith and in experience of its power, fulfilling together their witness and service to the world. At this point of locality there should be in evidence something of the meaning of the ecumenical movement as the pilgrimage of all Christ's people towards the wholeness of the Church, the fulfilment of its calling in the world and the realization of what the Christian society means in its temporal and eternal significance. What are some of the requisites if the local church is to correspond to this conception of its significance? Here are a few, out of many:

(i) Clergy and ministers, all who are responsible for leading and serving any company of Christ's people, should never lose sight of the vast and rich dimensions of their responsibilities. All forms of ordination to the Christian ministry imply—and usually make explicit—the fact that a local minister is a minister of the Church universal. In any given instance this claim within the divided state of the churches may be disputed. Universal agreement on the status of particular ordinations tarries but the vocation to ministering lies deeper than these disputes, and the minister knows it. He may not claim ecclesiastical prerogatives which are denied him by our divisions, but at the heart of his calling there is a commissioning which is not of his claiming; it is of Christ's bestowing. Nothing in the doctrine of the priesthood of all believers can weaken this special responsibility for leading and nurturing a local company of believers in the full dimensions of the Christian life and the Church catholic. When this responsibility is accepted and fulfilled with imagination, caring, and dedication, certain catholic notes become apparent in the conduct of worship, the content of preaching and teaching, and in every phase of leadership in service and outreach. The Christian ministry is an ecumenical ministry.

(ii) Every member of a local Christian congregation should realize—and be helped to realize—that membership in the Church is membership of the Church universal. Confirmation, reception into membership (whatever a particular denominational rite may be), is not the admission into some little niche, preferably a cosy and undemanding one, in a corner of the household of faith. It is entrance into the full and varied, the active and often tumultuous life of a worldwide community with a worldwide task. To be a member of a local church means—or ought to mean—being caught up into the ever-renewed life of the Church universal. Local membership is ecumenical membership, with costly but exhilarating participation in the movement.

(iii) At least one person, as well as the parson, needs to be made responsible in every congregation for ensuring that contacts are maintained with the sources of information concerning the Church throughout the world and the most significant contemporary aspects of the ecumenical movement. The World Council of Churches, national councils of churches, the missionary agencies and the Bible societies, publish in various forms news sheets, pamphlets, books, audio-visual aids, which provide this constant flow of information. The trouble is in the log-jam, the blocking or ignoring of the channels of information. How many parish magazines, denominational journals and such like, make imaginative use of this material? Are they almost exclusively parochial in the limited and limiting sense of the term, or are they organs of an exciting world movement in the greatest of all enterprises?

(iv) No local congregation can live to itself and still be in truth a Church. Ecumenical relationships begin with local relationships, and this at a depth far profounder than a few kind words from the vicar or a neighbouring Roman Catholic priest at the tea-table followed by a light-hearted response from the Free Church minister. There should be local engagement in, for example, joint Bible study, joint study groups (taking into their attention some of the more important—maybe controversial—events within the ecumenical movement); joint action in Christian aid, in local social action, in missionary outreach and in the imaginative use of the annual Weeks of Prayer for Christian Unity; the visitation of neighbouring churches and participation in their worship as well as local experiments in united worship, maybe using such contemporary forms as are available through various liturgical renewal groups. What matters in all this is alertness, imagination, and courage—the last often being necessary amidst the frustrations which can be occasioned by Gospel-hardened parishioners who would prefer the words 'Sleep on now and take your rest' to 'Take up your cross and follow me'.

When the fourth World Conference on Faith and Order in 1963

dispersed, its participants took home with them five questions with which they undertook to live, giving their affirmative answer and watching for its continuing implications. Every local church would do well to take the same course and reckon seriously and enthusiastically with these questions:

Will you join us in the attempt to submit all that our own churches mean to us, and all that we can understand of others, to the judgement of Christ, Lord of us all? This conception of our work as a going deep together is a new approach and is full of promise.

Will you try to understand other churches' history as deeply as your own? Thus we discover fellowship with other Christians throughout all time as well as through all the world. The Church, age-old as well as worldwide, may so learn more of him who is the God of ages.

Will you recognize that Christ calls the whole Church into his whole ministry, so that we may have a fresh understanding of the various ministries which he gives within the whole ministry?

Will you, as you worship God, seek to learn from other traditions more of what true worship is meant to be in all its depth and range, reflecting his presence in remembrance, communion and expectation and magnifying him in the glory and travail of his creation?

Will you humbly recognize that many of God's gifts to his whole Church cannot be shared by us in our local churches, until we become the one people of God in each place, and are prepared to realize this by new and bold ventures of living faith?[1]

Here is a prayer to be said by every local congregation in the faith that when the answer is given to the Church universal it will be experienced and demonstrated in every local church, to the delight and exhilaration of all its members and to the glory of the God and Father of our Lord Jesus Christ and our Father:

O Lord of the Church, make thy Church one and heal our divisions;

> make thy Church holy in all her members and in all her branches;

> make thy Church truly catholic—for all men and in all truth;

> make thy Church apostolic—give her the faith and missionary spirit of the first apostles;

and may the grace of our Lord Jesus Christ, the love of God and the fellowship of the Holy Spirit be with us all evermore.

---

[1] See the *Ecumenical Review*, October 1963, p. 106,

APPENDIXES

I   A Note on Sources

Two indispensable volumes are the *History of the Ecumenical Movement 1517–1948* by Ruth Rouse and S. C. Neill (London SPCK, 1954) and *The Ecumenical Advance; A History of the Ecumenical Movement, Vol. II, 1948–1968* (SPCK, 1970). Other detailed contributions to the history of the ecumenical movement, with special reference to Asia and North America, are Hans-Ruedi Weber, *Asia and the Ecumenical Movement 1895–1961* (London, SCM Press, 1966); Samuel McCrea Cavert, *The American Churches in the Ecumenical Movement 1900–1968* (New York, Association Press, 1968) and *Church Cooperation and Unity in America 1900–1970* (Association Press, 1970).

New Delhi to Uppsala 1961–1968 (Geneva, WCC) and *The Uppsala Report* edited by Norman Goodall (WCC) contain essential material from which many of the quotations in this volume have been taken. Two journals are of special importance—the *Ecumenical Review* (particularly for its Ecumenical Chronicle and Ecumenical Diary) and the *International Review of Mission* (reflecting the standpoint of the Commissions on World Mission and Evangelism). Both these journals are published quarterly by the WCC. *Study Encounter* and *Risk* (approximately quarterly since 1965) are further documentary sources and provide a forum for ecumenical debate. The *Interchurch Aid Newsletter* (approximately monthly) reports the far-reaching activities of the Commission on Inter-Church Aid, Refugee and World Service. *Ecumenical Press Service* is a news sheet of ecumenical events covering more than WCC activities. The *Minutes* of the WCC Central Committee contain the most authoritative and voluminous record of the Council's policy and administration. They are distributed to all member churches and a limited number are also on sale in Geneva. They include detailed reports of specialized and related agencies of the Council and summaries of the proceedings of the Joint Working Group with the Roman Catholic Church.

Roman Catholic journals concerned particularly with ecumenical matters include the *Heythrop Journal* (London, Heythrop College), *Istina* (Boulogne-sur-Seine), *The Month* (London), *The New Concilium* (New York) and *Irenicon* (Chevetogne). Specially valuable is the *Information Service* of the Vatican Secretariat for Promoting Christian Unity. The Second Vatican Council has given rise to an immense range of writings: a most useful basic volume is *The Documents of Vatican II*, edited by W. M. Abbot, which includes notes on the Documents and comments by Protestant and Orthodox scholars (London, Geoffrey Chapman, 1967).

Conservative evangelicalism is represented in *Christianity Today* (Washington) and *Idea* (Information Department of the Evangelical Alliance, London). The report of the Keele Conference of Evangelicals in 1967 is published by the Church Pastoral Aid Society, London, and should be read in conjunction with a preparatory volume *Guidelines* edited by J. I. Packer (1967).

Publications of the World Council of Churches (on which this book has greatly depended) include, in addition to the periodicals mentioned above, regular reports of commissions, consultations, working-parties etc. convened for the study of particular issues. Many of these publications pass too quickly into the oblivion of in-trays which are never emptied except when they are tipped into waste-paper baskets. Some of them record findings, reflections, and the results of research, which deserve a better fate and which should be used to inform and stimulate local churches concerning the realities of the ecumenical task. Such series as the reports and pamphlets of the Faith and Order Commission, research papers of the Commission on World Mission and Evangelism and documents on race, development, the challenge of technology, education, are of particular importance. Publications lists are issued regularly and may be obtained from the WCC Publications Office, 150 Route de Ferney, 1211 Geneva 20, Switzerland. Combined subscriptions covering periodicals are available.

For primary sources concerning the ecumenical movement the Library of the World Council in Geneva is a unique repository. In addition to more than 40,000 books and pamphlets and files of over 800 journals, the library houses the entire archives of the International Missionary Council from 1910 to 1961; those of Faith and Order since 1910, Life and Work since 1925, the World Student Christian Federation since the late nineteenth century and the World Alliance for Promoting International Friendship through the Churches (1914–1948). The Library is, of course, also the home of the World Council's archives since the years of its 'process of formation'. The Library is open to students and other visitors. Its Director is Dr. A. J. van der Bent.

II   A Chronology

1959

World Refugee Year

January   1st Conference of European Churches, Nyborg, Denmark

1 January   Fidel Castro assumed power in Cuba

14 January   Death of Bishop Eivind Berggrav

25 January   Pope John XXIII announced his intention to summon a 2nd Vatican Council

27 April   Death of Archbishop Ingve Brilioth

14–24 May   Inaugural Assembly of East Asia Christian Conference, Kuala Lumpur, Malaya

27 July–6 August   18th General Council of World Alliance of Reformed Churches, São Paulo, Brazil

24 October   Death of Walter Freytag

1960

3 May European Free Trade Association formed (EFTA) (following the creation of the European Economic Community 3 years previously)

30 June Independence of the Congo Republic: civil war

August Archbishop Makarios became President of an independent Cyprus

9 November John F. Kennedy became President of the U.S.A.

7–14 December The 'Cottesloe Consultation' Johannesburg; WCC consultation with member churches in South Africa

1961

14 March Publication of *The New English Bible* (New Testament)

22 April–4 May 1st Conference of Churches and Missions in the Pacific, leading to the subsequent formation of the Pacific Conference of Churches

31 May The Republic of South Africa left the Commonwealth

29 July–6 August Latin American Evangelical Conference, Lima, Peru

17 September Dag Hammerskjöld killed in a plane crash

November 3rd Assembly of the WCC, New Delhi, Integration of the International Missionary Council and the WCC. The Orthodox Church of Russia and two Pentecostal Churches became members

25 December Pope John XXIII issued apostolic constitution *Humanae Salutis* convoking the 2nd Vatican Council

The Dutch Reformed Church of the Transvaal and the Hervormde Kerk of South Africa withdrew from the WCC

The Berlin Wall was built

Publication of Gabriel Vahanian's *The Death of God* and of William Hamilton's *The New Essence of Christianity* (precipitating the 'Death of God' controversy)

1962

4–12 July 9th Assembly of the International Congregational Council, Rotterdam

11 September 2nd Vatican Council opened

1963

January 1st All Africa Christian Youth Assembly, Nairobi, Kenya

10 February Death of Adolf Keller

19 March Publication of John Robinson's *Honest to God*

20–30 April 1st All Africa Conference of Churches, Kampala, Uganda

4 May Pierre Benignus killed in a plane crash in the Camerouns

3 June Death of Pope John XXIII

July 4th World Conference on Faith and Order, Montreal, Canada

30 July–11 August Assembly of the Lutheran World Federation, Helsinki

22 November President Kennedy assassinated

4 December Vatican Council's promulgation of the Constitution on the Sacred Liturgy and the Decree on the Instruments of Social Communication

8–19 December   Meeting of the Commission on World Mission and Evangelism, Mexico
31 December   Dissolution of the Federation of Central Africa

1964

5 January   Pope Paul met the Ecumenical Patriarch Athenagoras in the Holy Land
1 February   Malawi assumed internal self-government
25 February–5 March   2nd Assembly of the East Asia Christian Conference, Bangkok
25 April   Tanzania became independent
3–13 August   19th General Council of the World Alliance of Reformed Churches
5–9 October   4th Conference of European Churches, Nyborg, Denmark
16 October   China exploded her first atom bomb
24 October   Zambia became independent
21 November   Vatican Council's promulgation of the Dogmatic Constitution on the Church, the Decree on Ecumenism, and the Decree on Eastern Catholic Churches. Pope Paul VI proclaimed the title of Mary as Mother of the Church

1965

15–21 January   Conference of Heads of Oriental Orthodox Churches (Egypt, Syria, Ethiopia, Armenia, and India) in Addis Ababa, the 'first since the Council of Chalcedon'
24 January   Death of Winston Churchill
7 February   U.S.A. began bombing military targets in North Vietnam
18 February   Announcement by Cardinal Bea that the Vatican had given consent to the establishment of a Joint Working Group between the WCC and the Roman Catholic Church
8 May   Death of Alphons Koechlin
11 July   Opening of the new Ecumenical Centre, Geneva
15 September   Pope Paul VI issued the apostolic constitution *Apostolica Sollicitudo* defining the purpose of the new Episcopal Synod
4 October   Pope Paul VI addressed the United Nations General Assembly in New York
11 November   Rhodesia made a Unilateral Declaration of Independence
11 November   Death of Hendrik Kraemer
18 November   Introduction of the process for the beatification of Popes Pius XII and John XXIII
During the final session of the Vatican Council the remaining Decrees, Declarations, and Pastoral Constitutions were promulgated, including those on Religious Freedom, the Church's Missionary Activity, the Relationship of the Church to non-Christian Religions, the Apostolate of the Laity
Centenary of the birth of John R. Mott

1966

19 January   Indira Gandhi became Prime Minister of India
24 February   Kwame Nkrumah of Ghana deposed and went into exile
23 March   The Archbishop of Canterbury visited Pope Paul VI in Rome
May   Inaugural Assembly of the Pacific Conference of Churches at Lifu, Loyalty Islands
26 May   Guyana became independent
10 July   10th Assembly of the International Congregational Council, Swansea
12–26 July   World Conference on Church and Society
18–26 August   11th World Methodist Conference, London
6 September   Prime Minister Verwoerd of South Africa assassinated
Centenary of the birth of Nathan Soderblöm

1967

18 January   Death of Berkelbach van der Sprenkel
31 January   Death of Bishop Otto Dibelius
22 February   Death of Leslie Cook
1 March   Death of Korula Jacob
26 March   Publication of the Papal encyclical *Populorum progressio*
4–7 April   Evangelical Anglican Conference, Keele
14 May   Publication (by the Vatican Secretariat for Promoting Christian Unity) of the Ecumenical Directory, giving guidance for applying the decisions of Vatican Council II on ecumenical matters 'with pastoral prudence' but 'without obstructing the ways of divine Providence and without pre-judging the future inspirations of the Holy Spirit'
5–10 June   The 'six-day' war in the Middle East
6 June   Death of Philippe Maury
29 July–8 August   Meeting of the Faith and Order Commission, Bristol
September   Death of Chief Albert Luthuli
29 September–29 October   1st Meeting of the Roman Catholic Synod of Bishops
29 September–6 October   5th Conference of European Churches, Nyborg
11–18 October   3rd World Congress of the Lay Apostolate of the Roman Catholic Church
31 October   Service held in Wittenberg to celebrate the 450th Anniversary of the Reformation
1st week in November   Visit of the Ecumenical Patriarch Athenagoras I to the Ecumenical Centre, Geneva
Civil war in Nigeria

1968

30 January–8 February   4th Assembly of the East Asia Christian Conference, Bangkok
February   Death of F. M. Baron von Asbeck
4 April   Assassination of Martin Luther King
11 May   Death of Z. K. Matthews

2 June   Publication under the joint auspices of the United Bible Societies
and the Vatican Secretariat for Promoting Christian Unity of 'Guiding
Principles for inter-confessional co-operation in translating the Bible'
5 June   Assassination of Senator Robert Kennedy
6 June   Death of Franklin Clark Fry
4–19 July   4th Assembly of the World Council of Churches, Uppsala
25 July–25 August   The 10th Lambeth Conference of Bishops
November   Death of Augustin Cardinal Bea
9 December   Death of Karl Barth
21–27 December   Three astronauts in Apollo 8 made ten orbits round the
moon

1969

17 January   Death of Kenneth Scott Latourette
16 May   Death of J. H. Oldham
June   Militant 'Black Power' groups in the U.S.A. 'liberate' the Inter-
Church Centre, New York, and sundry churches, demanding 'repara-
tions'
10 June   Visit of Pope Paul VI to the Ecumenical Centre, Geneva
14 August   Death of Hamilcar Alivisatos
1–12 September   2nd Assembly of the All Africa Conference of Churches,
Abidjan, Ivory Coast
26 December   Death of Josef L. Hromadka

1970

15 January   End of Nigerian civil war
16 March   Publication of *The New English Bible* (Old Testament), com-
pleting the translation
14–24 July   5th Assembly of the Lutheran World Federation
15 August   WCC's 'Programme to Combat Racism' launched
20–30 August   Uniting Assembly of the World Alliance of Reformed
Churches and the International Congregational Council, Nairobi
20 December   Death of Marc Boegner

1971

26 April–3 May   6th Conference of European Churches, Nyborg
1 June   Death of Reinhold Niebuhr
June   3rd Assembly of the Pacific Conference of Churches, Davuilevu,
near Suva
July   Assembly of the World Council of Christian Education; approval
given to proposed integration with the WCC
2–13 August   Meeting of Faith and Order Commission, Louvain
Civil War in Pakistan

III World Council of Churches

(a) *Officers and Members of the Executive Committee*
(as at March 1972)

Honorary President
Rev. Dr. W. A. Visser 't Hooft — Netherlands Reformed Church

Presidium

Dr. (Mrs.) K. T. Cho	United Church of Christ in Japan
His Holiness Patriarch German of Serbia	Serbian Orthodox Church
Rt. Rev. Bishop Hanns Lilje	Evangelical Church in Germany (Lutheran)
Rev. Dr. E. A. Payne	The Baptist Union of Great Britain and Ireland
Rev. Dr. J. C. Smith	The United Presbyterian Church in the U.S.A.
Rt. Rev. A. H. Zulu, Bishop of Zululand	Church of the Province of South Africa

Chairman
Dr. M. M. Thomas — Mar Thoma Syrian Orthodox Church of Malabar

Vice-Chairman

Metropolitan Meliton of Chalcedon	Ecumenical Patriarchate of Constantinople
Miss P. M. Webb	The Methodist Church, U.K.

Chairman of Finance Committee
The Rt. Hon. The Earl of March — Church of England

General Secretary
Rev. Dr. E. C. Blake — The United Presbyterian Church in the U.S.A.

Members of Executive Committee

Rev. J. B. Bokeleale	Disciples of Christ in the Congo
Mr. J. V. Faune	United Church of Christ in the Philippines
President K. Gottschald	Evangelical Church of Lutheran Confession in Brazil
Mr. D. E. Johnson	Episcopal Church, U.S.A.
Most Rev. Archbishop Ruben Josefson	Church of Sweden
Professor Dr. J. M. Lochman	Evangelical Church of Czech Brethren

Rev. Dr. R. J. Marshall	Lutheran Church in America
Bishop Dr. R. C. Nichols	The Methodist Church, U.S.A.
Metropolitan Nikodim of Leningrad and Novgorod	Orthodox Church of Russia
Rev. Dr. Jacques Rossel	Swiss Protestant Church Federation
Professor T. Sabev	Bulgarian Orthodox Church
Bishop K. Sarkissian	Armenian Apostolic Church
General T. B. Simatupang	Indonesian Christian Church
Dr. R. von Weizsäcker	Evangelical Church in Germany (United)
Mrs. Janet Wesonga	Church of Uganda

(b) *Member Churches of the World Council of Churches*
(as at the close of 1971. The dates in brackets indicate the year in which the church became a member.)

Argentina
IGLESIA EVANGELICA DEL RIO DE LA PLATA (1956)
(Evangelical Church of the River Plate)

THE EVANGELICAL METHODIST CHURCH OF ARGENTINA (1971)[1]

Australasia
METHODIST CHURCH OF AUSTRALASIA (1946)
THE UNITED CHURCH OF PAPUA, NEW GUINEA AND THE SOLOMON ISLANDS (1971)

Australia
CHURCHES OF CHRIST IN AUSTRALIA (1941)
THE CHURCH OF ENGLAND IN AUSTRALIA (1940)
CONGREGATIONAL UNION OF AUSTRALIA (1945)
PRESBYTERIAN CHURCH OF AUSTRALIA (1938)

Austria
ALT-KATHOLISCHE KIRCHE ÖSTERREICHS (1967)
(Old Catholic Church of Austria)

EVANGELISCHE KIRCHE A.U.H.B. IN ÖSTERREICH (1946)
(Evangelical Church of the Augsburg and Helvetic Confession)

Belgium
ÉGLISE PROTESTANTE DE BELGIQUE (1945)
(Protestant Church of Belgium)

[1] Formerly in membership through the United Methodist Church, U.S.A., (q.v.).

ÉGLISE REFORMÉE DE BELGIQUE (1939)[2]
(Reformed Church of Belgium)

Brazil
IGREJA EPISCOPAL DO BRASIL (1966)
(Episcopal Church of Brazil)

IGREJA EVANGELICA DE CONFISSAO LUTHERANA NO BRASIL (1950)
(Evangelical Church of Lutheran Confession in Brazil)

IGREJA EVANGELICA PENTECOSTAL 'O BRASIL PARA CRISTO' (1969)
(Evangelical Pentecostal Church 'Brazil for Christ')

IGREJA METODISTA DO BRASIL (1942)
(Methodist Church of Brazil)

Bulgaria
ÉGLISE ORTHODOXE DE BULGARIE (1961)
(Bulgarian Orthodox Church)

Burma
BURMA BAPTIST CONVENTION (1957)
THE CHURCH OF THE PROVINCE OF BURMA (1971)[3]

Cameroon
ÉGLISE ÉVANGÉLIQUE DU CAMEROUN (1958)
(Evangelical Church of Cameroon)

ÉGLISE PRESBYTERIENNE CAMEROUNAISE (1963)
(Presbyterian Church of Cameroon)

PRESBYTERIAN CHURCH IN WEST CAMEROON (1961)

UNION DES ÉGLISES BAPTISTES DU CAMEROUN (1961)
(Union of Baptist Churches of Cameroon)

Canada
THE ANGLICAN CHURCH OF CANADA (1939)
CANADIAN YEARLY MEETING OF THE SOCIETY OF FRIENDS (1942)
CHURCHES OF CHRIST (DISCIPLES) (1947)
THE EVANGELICAL LUTHERAN CHURCH OF CANADA (1967)
THE PRESBYTERIAN CHURCH IN CANADA (1940)
THE UNITED CHURCH OF CANADA (1938)

Central Africa
CHURCH OF THE PROVINCE OF CENTRAL AFRICA (1956)
UNITED CHURCH OF ZAMBIA (1966)

[2] Formerly Belgian Christian Missionary Council.
[3] Formerly in membership through the Church of India, Pakistan, Burma and Ceylon (1939).

Ceylon
METHODIST CHURCH, CEYLON (1950)
(See also under Church of India, Pakistan and Ceylon)

Chile
IGLESIA EVANGÉLICA LUTHERANA EN CHILE (1965)
(Evangelical–Lutheran Church in Chile)

IGLESIA PENTECOSTAL DE CHILE (1961)
(Pentecostal Church of Chile)

MISSION IGLESIA PENTECOSTAL (1961)
(Pentecostal Mission Church)

China
CHINA BAPTIST COUNCIL (1946)

CHUNG-HUA CHI-TU CHIAO-HUI (1939)
(Church of Christ in China)

CHING-HUA SHENG KUNG HUI (1947)
(Anglican Church in China)

HUA PEI KUNG LI HUI (1947)
(North China Congregational Church)

Congo (Brazzaville)
ÉGLISE ÉVANGÉLIQUE DU CONGO (1963)
(Evangelical Church of the Congo)

Congo (Kinshasa)
ÉGLISE DU CHRIST AU CONGO (DISCIPLES DU CHRIST) (1965)
(Church of Christ in Congo—Disciples of Christ)

ÉGLISE DU CHRIST SUR LA TERRE PAR LE PROPHÈTE SIMON KIMBANGU (1969)
(Church of Christ on Earth by the Prophet Simon Kimbangu)

ÉGLISE ÉVANGÉLIQUE DU CONGO KINSHASA (1961)
(Evangelical Church of Congo Kinshasa)

Cyprus
CHURCH OF CYPRUS (1946)

Czechoslovakia
CESKOBRATRSKA CIRKEV EVANGELICKA (1935)
(Evangelical Church of Czech Brethren)

CESKOSLOVENSKA CIRKEV (1963)
(Czechoslovak Church)

EVANGELICKA CIRKEV A.V. NA SLOVENSKU (1946)
(Evangelical Church in Czechoslovakia, Augsburg Confession)

ORTHODOX CHURCH OF CZECHOSLOVAKIA (1966)

REF. KREST. CIRKVI NA SLOVENSKU (1946)
(Reformed Christian Church in Slovakia)

SLEZSKA CIRKEV EVANGELICKA A.V. (1955)
(Evangelical Church of the Augsburg Confession in Silesia)

Denmark

BAPTIST UNION OF DENMARK (1945)

DEN EVANGELISKLUTHERSKE FOLKEKIRKE I DANMARK (1940)
(Church of Denmark)

East Africa (See also Kenya, Uganda, Tanzania)

THE PRESBYTERIAN CHURCH OF EAST AFRICA (1957)

Egypt

COPTIC EVANGELICAL CHURCH—THE SYNDOD OF THE NILE (1963)

COPTIC ORTHODOX CHURCH (1948)

GREEK ORTHODOX PATRIARCHATE OF ALEXANDRIA (1948)

Estonia

EESTI EVANGELTUMI LUTERI USU KIRIK (1938)[4]
(Estonian Evangelical Lutheran Church)

Ethiopia

ETHIOPIAN ORTHODOX CHURCH (1948)

Finland

SUOMEN EVANKELIS–LUTERILAINEN KIRKKO (1938)
(Evangelical Church of Finland)

France

ÉGLISE DE LA CONFESSION D'AUGSBOURG D'ALSACE ET DE LORRAINE (1947)
(Evangelical Church of the Augsburg Confession in Alsace and Lorraine)

ÉGLISE ÉVANGÉLIQUE LUTHÉRIENNE DE FRANCE (1946)
(Evangelical Lutheran Church of France)

ÉGLISE REFORMÉE D'ALSACE ET DE LORRAINE (1939)
(Reformed Church of Alsace and Lorraine)

ÉGLISE REFORMÉE DE FRANCE (1939)
(Reformed Church of France)

Gabon

ÉGLISE ÉVANGÉLIQUE DU GABON (1961)
(Evangelical Church of Gabon)

[4] This Church is composed of congregations, originally refugees or in exile from their historic 'mother church' in the U.S.S.R. and now settled in other countries.

Germany
Federal Republic of Germany
ALT-KATHOLISCHE KIRCHE IN DEUTSCHLAND (1947)
(Old Catholic Church in Germany)

EVANGELISCHE BRÜDER-UNITÄT (1947)
(Moravian Church)

EVANGELISCHE KIRCHE IN DEUTSCHLAND (1945)
    EVANGELISCHE KIRCHE IN BERLIN-BRANDENBURG (West)
    EVANGELISCHE KIRCHE VON WESTFALEN
    EVANGELISCHE KIRCHE IM RHEINLAND
    EVANGELISCH–LUTHERISCHE LANDESKIRCHE HANNOVERS[5]
    EVANGELISCH–LUTHERISCHE KIRCHE IN BAYERN[5]
    EVANGELISCH–LUTHERISCHE LANDESKIRCHE SCHLESWIG–HOLSTEINS[5]
    EVANGELISCH–LUTHERISCHE KIRCHE IM HAMBURGISCHEN STAATE[5]
    EVANGELISCH–LUTHERISCHE LANDESKIRCHE IN BRAUNSCHWEIG[5]
    EVANGELISCH–LUTHERISCHE KIRCHE IN LÜBECK[5]
    EVANGELISCH–LUTHERISCHE LANDESKIRCHE V. SCHAUMBURG–LIPPE[5]
    EVANGELISCHE LANDESKIRCHE IN WÜRTTEMBERG
    EVANGELISCH–LUTHERISCHE KIRCHE IN OLDENBURG
    EVANGELISCH–LUTHERISCHE LANDESKIRCHE EUTIN[5]
    EVANGELISCHE KIRCHE IN HESSEN UND NASSAU
    EVANGELISCHE KIRCHE VON KURHESSEN–WALDECK
    EVANGELISCHE LANDESKIRCHE IN BADEN
    VEREINIGTE PROTESTANTISCH–EVANGELISCH–CHRISTLICHE KIRCHE DER PFALZ
    BREMISCHE EVANGELISCHE KIRCHE
    EVANGELISCH–REFORMIERTE KIRCHE IN NORDWESTDEUTSCHLAND
    LIPPISCHE LANDESKIRCHE

VEREINIGUNG DER DEUTSCHEN MENNONITENGEMEINDEN (Mennonite Church)

[5] This Church is directly a member of the World Council of Churches in accordance with the resolution of the General Synod of the United Evangelical Lutheran Church of Germany, dated 27 January 1949, which recommended that the member churches of the United Evangelical Lutheran Church should make the following declaration to the Council of the Evangelical Church in Germany concerning their relation to the World Council of Churches:

'The Evangelical Church in Germany has made it clear through its constitution that it is a federation (Bund) of confessionally determined churches. Moreover, the conditions of membership of the World Council of Churches have been determined at the Assembly at Amsterdam. Therefore, this Evangelical Lutheran Church declares concerning its membership in the World Council of Churches:

(i) It is represented in the World Council as a church of the Evangelical Lutheran confession.

(ii) Representatives which it sends to the World Council are to be identified as Evangelical Lutherans.

(iii) Within the limits of the competence of the Evangelical Church in Germany it is represented in the World Council through the intermediary of the Council of the Evangelical Church in Germany.'

German Democratic Republic

GEMEINDEVERBAND DER ALT-KATHOLISCHEN KIRCHE IN DER DEUTSCHEN DEMOKRATISCHEN REPUBLIK (Federation of the Old Catholic Church in the German Democratic Republic)

BUND DER EVANGELISCHEN KIRCHEN IN DER DEUTSCHEN DEMOKRATISCHEN REPUBLIK (Federation of the Evangelical Churches in the German Democratic Republic)

EVANGELISCHE KIRCHE IN BERLIN–BRANDENBURG (East)[6]
EVANGELISCHE LANDESKIRCHE GREIFSWALD[6]
EVANGELISCHE KIRCHE DES GORLITZER KIRCHENGEBIETES[6]
EVANGELISCHE KIRCHE DER KIRCHENPROVINZ SACHSEN[6]
EVANGELISCH–LUTHERISCHE LANDESKIRCHE SACHSENS[6]
EVANGELISCH–LUTHERISCHE KIRCHE IN THÜRINGEN[6]
EVANGELISCH–LUTHERISCHE LANDESKIRCHE MECKLENBURGS[6]
EVANGELISCHE LANDESKIRCHE ANHALTS[6]
EVANGELISCHE BRÜDER–UNITÄT (DISTRIKT HERRNHUT)

Ghana

EVANGELICAL PRESBYTERIAN CHURCH (1963)
THE METHODIST CHURCH, GHANA (1960)
PRESBYTERIAN CHURCH OF GHANA (1953)
THE CHURCH OF THE PROVINCE OF WEST AFRICA (q.v.)

Greece

EKKLESIA TES ELLADOS (1947)
(Church of Greece)

GREEK EVANGELICAL CHURCH (1947)

Hong Kong

THE CHURCH OF CHRIST IN CHINA, THE HONG KONG COUNCIL (1967)

Hungary

MAGYARORSZAGI BAPTISTA EGYHAZ (1956)
(Baptist Church of Hungary)

MAGYARORSZAGI EVANGELIKUS EGYHAZ (1943)
(Lutheran Church of Hungary)

MAGYARORSZAGI REFORMATUS EGYHAZ (1940)
(Reformed Church of Hungary)

Iceland

EVANGELICAL LUTHERAN CHURCH OF ICELAND (1948)

[6] United in a fellowship of Christian witness and service in the Federation of Evangelical Churches in the German Democratic Republic (GDR), these churches are represented in the Council through agencies of the Federation of Evangelical Churches in the GDR.

India
CHURCH OF INDIA, PAKISTAN AND CEYLON (1939)[7]
CHURCH OF NORTH INDIA (1971)[8]
CHURCH OF SOUTH INDIA (1948)
FEDERATION OF EVANGELICAL LUTHERAN CHURCHES IN INDIA (1946)
MAR THOMA SYRIAN CHURCH OF MALABAR (1939)
THE ORTHODOX SYRIAN CHURCH OF THE EAST (1947)
THE SAMAVESAM OF TELUGU BAPTIST CHURCHES (1965)

Indonesia
GEREDJA BATAK KARO PROTESTANT (1969)
(Karo Batak Protestant Church)

GEREDJA GEREDJA KRISTEN DJAWA DI DJAWA TENGAH (1950)
(Christian Churches of Mid-Java)

GEREDJA KALIMANTAN EVANGELIS (1948)
(Kalimantan Evangelical Church)

GEREDJA KRISTEN DJAWA WETAN (1945)
(Christian Church of East Java)

GEREDJA KRISTEN INDJILI DI IRIAN BARAT (1967)
(Evangelical Christian Church in West Irian)

GEREDJA KRISTEN INDONESIA (1965)
(Indonesia Christian Church)

GEREDJA KRISTEN PASUNDAN (1960)
(Sudanese Protestant Church of West Java)

GEREDJA KRISTEN SULAWESI TENGAH (1948)
(Christian Church in Mid-Sulawesi)

GEREDJA MASEHI INDJILI MINAHASA (1948)
(Christian Evangelical Church in Minahasa)

GEREDJA MASEHI INDJILI DI TIMOR (1948)
(Protestant Evangelical Church in Timor)

GEREDJA PROTESTAN DI INDONESIA (1939)
(Protestant Church in Indonesia)

[7] Formerly the Church of India, Pakistan, Burma, and Ceylon. The Church of the Province of Burma is now a member in its own right. The North India and Pakistan dioceses are part of the Church of North India and Pakistan respectively. If, as is expected, the Ceylon diocese becomes part of the united Church in 1972, the term 'Church of India, Pakistan, and Ceylon' will disappear, all its component parts having become members of the WCC in their new status.

[8] An enlarged union of churches in North India including the former United Church of Northern India (1947), the North India dioceses of the Church of India, Pakistan and Ceylon, the Council of Baptist Churches in North India, the Disciples of Christ, and the Methodist Church (British and Australasian Conferences).

GEREDJA PROTESTAN MALUKU (1948)
(Protestant Church of the Moluccas)

GEREDJA TORADJA (1967)
(Toradja Church)

HURIA KRISTEN BATAK PROTESTAN (1948)
(Protestant Christian Batak Church)

Iran
SYNOD OF THE EVANGELICAL CHURCH OF IRAN (1950)

Italy
CHIESA EVANGELICA METODISTA D'ITALIA (1947)
(Evangelical Methodist Church of Italy)

CHIESA EVANGELICA VALDESE (1945)
(Waldensian Church)

Jamaica
THE MORAVIAN CHURCH IN JAMAICA (1969)
THE UNITED CHURCH OF JAMAICA AND GRAND CAYMAN (1967)

Japan
NIPPON KIRISUTO KYODAN (1948)
(The United Church of Christ in Japan)

NIPPON SEI KO KAI (1948)
(Anglican Episcopal Church in Japan)

Jerusalem
GREEK ORTHODOX PATRIARCHATE OF JERUSALEM (1946)

Kenya (See also East Africa)
THE CHURCH OF THE PROVINCE OF KENYA (1971)[9]
THE METHODIST CHURCH IN KENYA (1968)
THE PRESBYTERIAN CHURCH OF EAST AFRICA (q.v.)

Korea
THE KOREAN METHODIST CHURCH (1947)
THE PRESBYTERIAN CHURCH IN THE REPUBLIC OF KOREA (1960)
THE PRESBYTERIAN CHURCH IN KOREA (1947)

Latvia
LATVIAN EVANGELICAL LUTHERAN CHURCH (1971)[10]

---

[9] Formerly part of the Church of the Province of East Africa (q.v.).
[10] This Church is composed of congregations, originally refugees or in exile from their historic 'mother church' in the U.S.S.R., and now settled in other countries.

Lebanon
ARMENIAN APOSTOLIC CHURCH (1962)
THE NATIONAL EVANGELICAL SYNOD OF SYRIA AND LEBANON (1946)[11]
UNION OF THE ARMENIAN EVANGELICAL CHURCHES IN THE NEAR EAST (1947)

Lesotho
LESOTHO EVANGELICAL CHURCH (1965)

Madagascar
ÉGLISE DE JESUS CHRIST A MADAGASCAR (1969)[12]
(Church of Jesus Christ in Madagascar)
ÉGLISE LUTHÉRIENNE MALGACHE (1966)

Malaysia
THE METHODIST CHURCH IN MALAYSIA AND SINGAPORE (1971)[13]

Mexico
IGLESIA METODISTA DE MEJICO (1940)
(Methodist Church of Mexico)

Netherlands
ALGEMENE DOOPSGEZINDE SOCIËTEIT (1939)
(General Mennonite Society)

EVANGELISCH–LUTHERSE KERK (1939)
(Evangelical Lutheran Church)

GEREFORMEERDE KERKEN IN NEDERLANDS (1971)
(Reformed Churches in the Netherlands)

NEDERLANDSE HERVORMDE KERK (1939)
(Netherlands Reformed Church)

OUD-KATHOLIEKE KERKE VAN NEDERLAND (1938)
(Old Catholic Church of the Netherlands)

REMONSTRANTSE BROEDERSCHAP (1939)
(Remonstrant Brotherhood)

New Caledonia
ÉGLISE ÉVANGÉLIQUE EN NOUVELLE–CALÉDONIE ET AUX ÎLES LOYAUTÉ (1961)
(Evangelical Church in New Caledonia and the Loyalty Isles)

New Hebrides
PRESBYTERIAN CHURCH OF THE NEW HEBRIDES (1961)

[11] See also Syria.
[12] Uniting the Church of Christ in Madagascar (1960), Malagasy Friends
Church (1967) and Evangelical Church of Madagascar (1960).
[13] Formerly in membership through the United Methodist Church, U.S.A.
(q.v.).

New Zealand
ASSOCIATED CHURCHES OF CHRIST IN NEW ZEALAND (1947)
THE BAPTIST UNION OF NEW ZEALAND (1944)
CHURCH OF THE PROVINCE OF NEW ZEALAND (ANGLICAN) (1942)
THE CONGREGATIONAL UNION OF NEW ZEALAND (1948)
THE METHODIST CHURCH OF NEW ZEALAND (1946)
THE PRESBYTERIAN CHURCH OF NEW ZEALAND (1940)

Nigeria (See also West Africa)
THE NIGERIAN BAPTIST CONVENTION (1971)
METHODIST CHURCH OF NIGERIA (1963)
THE PRESBYTERIAN CHURCH OF NIGERIA (1961)
THE CHURCH OF THE PROVINCE OF WEST AFRICA (q.v.)

Norway
NORSKE KIRKE (1948)
(Church of Norway)

Pakistan
THE CHURCH OF PAKISTAN (1971)[14]
(See also the Church of India, Pakistan, and Ceylon)

Philippines
IGLESIA FILIPINA INDEPENDIENTE (1958)
(Philippine Independent Church)
UNITED CHURCH OF CHRIST IN THE PHILIPPINES (1939)

Poland
ÉGLISE AUTOCEPH. ORTHODOXE EN POLOGNE (1961)
(Orthodox Church of Poland)

KOSCIOL EWANGELICKO–AUGSBURSKI W POLSCE (1938)
(Evangelical Church of the Augsburg Confession in Poland)

KOSCIOL POLSKOKATOLICKI W.P.R.L. (1948)
(Polish–Catholic Church in Poland)

STARO–KATOLICKIEGO KOSCIOLA MARIAWITOW W.P.R.L. (1969)
(Old Catholic Mariavite Church in Poland)

Romania
EVANGELICAL SYNODAL PRESBYTERIAL CHURCH OF THE AUGSBURG CONFESSION
IN THE SOCIALIST REPUBLIC OF ROMANIA (1948)
BISERICA EVANGELICA DUPA CONFESIUNEA DELA AUGSBURG (1947)
(Evangelical Church of the Augsburg Confession)

BISERICA ORTODOXA ROMANE (1961)
(Romanian Orthodox Church)

[14] Includes the former United Presbyterian Church of Pakistan (1961).

BISERICA REFORMATA DIN ROMANIA (1947)
(Reformed Church of Romania)

Samoa
CONGREGATIONAL CHRISTIAN CHURCH IN SAMOA (1961)

Sierra Leone
THE METHODIST CHURCH SIERRA LEONE (1967)

South Africa
THE BANTU PRESBYTERIAN CHURCH OF SOUTH AFRICA (1954)
CHURCH OF THE PROVINCE OF SOUTH AFRICA (1947)
EVANGELICAL LUTHERAN CHURCH IN SOUTHERN AFRICA—SOUTH-EASTERN
REGION (1962)
EVANGELICAL LUTHERAN CHURCH IN SOUTHERN AFRICA—TRANSVAAL REGION
(1968)
THE METHODIST CHURCH OF SOUTH AFRICA (1948)
MORAVIAN CHURCH IN SOUTH AFRICA—EASTERN PROVINCE (1968)
MORAVIAN CHURCH IN SOUTH AFRICA—WESTERN CAPE PROVINCE (1961)
THE PRESBYTERIAN CHURCH OF SOUTHERN AFRICA (1948)
THE UNITED CONGREGATIONAL CHURCH OF SOUTHERN AFRICA (1968)

Spain
IGLESIA EVANGELICA ESPAÑOLA (1947)
(Spanish Evangelical Church)

Sweden
SVENSKA KYRKAN (1939)
(Church of Sweden)

SVENSKA MISSIONSFÖRBUNDET (1946)
(The Mission Covenant Church of Sweden)

Switzerland
CHRISTKATHOLISCHE KIRCHE DER SCHWEIZ (1938)
(Old Catholic Church of Switzerland)

SCHWEIZERISCHER EVANGELISCHE KIRCHENBUND—FÉDÉRATION DES
ÉGLISES PROTESTANTES DE LA SUISSE (1940)
(Swiss Protestant Church Federation)

Syria
THE NATIONAL EVANGELICAL SYNOD OF SYRIA AND LEBANON (1948)[15]
PATRIARCAT GREC–ORTHODOXE D'ANTIOCHE ET DE TOUT L'ORIENT (1947)
(Greek Orthodox Patriarchate of Antioch and All the East)
SYRIAN ORTHODOX PATRIARCHATE OF ANTIOCH AND ALL THE EAST (1960)

[15] See also Lebanon.

Tahiti
ÉGLISE ÉVANGÉLIQUE DE POLYNESIE FRANÇAISE (1963)
(Evangelical Church of French Polynesia)

Taiwan
TAI-OAN KI-TOK TUI-LO KAU-HOE (1951)
(The Presbyterian Church of Formosa)

Tanzania (See also East Africa)
THE CHURCH OF THE PROVINCE OF TANZANIA (1971)[16]
EVANGELICAL LUTHERAN CHURCH IN TANZANIA (1967)

Togo
ÉGLISE ÉVANGÉLIQUE DU TOGO (1960)
(Evangelical Church of Togo)

Trinidad
THE PRESBYTERIAN CHURCH IN TRINIDAD AND GRENADA (1961)

Turkey
ECUMENICAL PATRIARCHATE OF CONSTANTINOPLE (1947)

Uganda
THE CHURCH OF UGANDA, RWANDA AND BURUNDI (1961)

Union of Soviet Socialist Republics
ARMENIAN APOSTOLIC CHURCH (1962)
ESTONIAN EVANGELICAL LUTHERAN CHURCH (1962)
EVANGELICAL LUTHERAN CHURCH OF LATVIA (1963)
GEORGIAN ORTHODOX CHURCH (1963)
ORTHODOX CHURCH OF RUSSIA (1961)
THE UNION OF EVANGELICAL CHRISTIAN BAPTISTS OF USSR (1962)

United Kingdom and Eire
THE BAPTIST UNION OF GREAT BRITAIN AND IRELAND (1939)
CHURCHES OF CHRIST IN GREAT BRITAIN AND IRELAND (1938)
CHURCH OF ENGLAND (1940)
CHURCH OF IRELAND (1943)
THE CHURCH OF SCOTLAND (1939)
CHURCH IN WALES (1947)
THE CONGREGATIONAL CHURCH IN ENGLAND AND WALES (1939)
THE CONGREGATIONAL UNION OF SCOTLAND (1940)
EPISCOPAL CHURCH IN SCOTLAND (1939)
THE METHODIST CHURCH (1948)
METHODIST CHURCH IN IRELAND (1939)
THE MORAVIAN CHURCH IN GREAT BRITAIN AND IRELAND (1949)
PRESBYTERIAN CHURCH OF ENGLAND (1939)

[16] Formerly part of the Church of the Province of East Africa (1960).

THE PRESBYTERIAN CHURCH IN IRELAND (1939)
THE PRESBYTERIAN CHURCH OF WALES (1947)
THE SALVATION ARMY (1939)
UNION OF WELSH INDEPENDENTS (1967)
UNITED FREE CHURCH OF SCOTLAND (1947)

United States of America

AFRICAN METHODIST EPISCOPAL CHURCH (1939)
AFRICAN METHODIST EPISCOPAL ZION CHURCH (1947)
AMERICAN BAPTIST CONVENTION (1939)
AMERICAN LUTHERAN CHURCH (1947)
ANTIOCHAN ORTHODOX CHRISTIAN ARCHDIOCESE (1939)
CHRISTIAN CHURCH (DISCIPLES OF CHRIST) (1938)
CHRISTIAN METHODIST EPISCOPAL CHURCH (1948)
CHURCH OF THE BRETHREN (1941)
EPISCOPAL CHURCH (1938)
HOLY APOSTOLIC CHURCH OF THE EAST (1943)
THE HUNGARIAN REFORMED CHURCH IN AMERICA (1958)
LUTHERAN CHURCH IN AMERICA (1962)[17]
THE MORAVIAN CHURCH IN AMERICA (NORTHERN PROVINCE) (1941)
MORAVIAN CHURCH IN AMERICA (SOUTHERN PROVINCE) (1953)
NATIONAL BAPTIST CONVENTION OF AMERICA (1955)
THE NATIONAL BAPTIST CONVENTION, U.S.A., INC. (1941)
POLISH NATIONAL CATHOLIC CHURCH OF AMERICA (1938)
THE PRESBYTERIAN CHURCH IN THE UNITED STATES (1939)
PROTESTANT EPISCOPAL CHURCH (1938)
REFORMED CHURCH IN AMERICA (1939)
RELIGIOUS SOCIETY OF FRIENDS
    FRIENDS GENERAL CONFERENCE (1941)
    FRIENDS UNITED MEETING (1940)
THE ROMANIAN ORTHODOX EPISCOPATE OF AMERICA (1938)
SEVENTH DAY BAPTIST GENERAL CONFERENCE (1939)
UNITED CHURCH OF CHRIST (CONGREGATIONAL CHRISTIAN CHURCHES; EVANGELICAL AND REFORMED CHURCH) (1961)
THE UNITED METHODIST CHURCH (1969)[18]
UNITED PRESBYTERIAN CHURCH OF THE USA (1958)

West Africa (see also Nigeria)

THE CHURCH OF THE PROVINCE OF WEST AFRICA (1953)

West Indies

CHURCH OF THE PROVINCE OF THE WEST INDIES (1939)
THE METHODIST CHURCH IN THE CARIBBEAN AND THE AMERICAS (1967)
MORAVIAN CHURCH (EASTERN WEST INDIES PROVINCE) (1971)

[17] This now includes the former American Evangelical Lutheran Church (1944), the Augustana Evangelical Lutheran Church (1941) and the Finnish Evangelical Lutheran Church of America (Suomi Synod) (1961).

[18] Union of the Methodist Church (1940) and the Evangelical United Brethren Church (1947).

Yugoslavia
REFORMED CHRISTIAN CHURCH OF YUGOSLAVIA (1948)
SERBIAN ORTHODOX CHURCH (1965)
SLOVAK EVANGELICAL CHURCH OF THE AUGSBURG CONFESSION IN YUGOSLAVIA (1963)

Zambia
UNITED CHURCH OF ZAMBIA (1966)

(c) *Associate Member Churches*

(These are churches which fulfil the criteria for membership except the requirement that 'a member church must ordinarily have at least 25,000 members'. Associate churches may send representatives to the Assembly with the right to speak but not to vote.)

Argentina
IGLESIA EVANGELICA LUTERANA UNIDA (1969)
(United Evangelical Lutheran Church)

Bolivia
THE METHODIST IN BOLIVIA (1971)[19]

Cameroon
ÉGLISE PROTESTANTE AFRICAINE (1968)
(African Protestant Church)

Chile
THE METHODIST CHURCH OF CHILE

Cuba
IGLESIA METODISTA EN CUBA (1968)
(Methodist Church in Cuba)
IGLESIA PRESBITERIANA–REFORMADA EN CUBA (1967)
(Presbyterian–Reformed Church in Cuba)

India
BENGAL–ORISSA–BIHAR BAPTIST CONVENTION (1965)

Japan
THE KOREAN CHRISTIAN CHURCH IN JAPAN (1963)

Liberia
PRESBYTERIAN CHURCH OF LIBERIA (1969)

[19] Formerly in membership through the United Methodist Church, U.S.A. (q.v.).

Netherlands Antilles
PROTESTANTSE KERK VAN DE NEDERLANDSE ANTILLEN (1969)[20]
(Protestant Church of the Netherlands Antilles)

Portugal
IGREJA EVANGELICA PRESBITERIANA DE PORTUGAL (1965)
(Evangelical Presbyterian Church of Portugal)

IGREJA LUSITANA CATOLICA APOSTOLICA EVANGELICA (1962)
(Lusitanian Church, Portugal)

Spain
IGLESIA ESPANOLA REFORMADA EPISCOPAL (1962)
(Spanish Reformed Episcopal Church)

Sudan
THE PRESBYTERIAN CHURCH IN THE SUDAN

Uruguay
THE EVANGELICAL METHODIST CHURCH IN URUGUAY (1971)[21]

West Africa
THE EVANGELICAL PRESBYTERIAN CHURCH IN RIO MUNI (1965)

(d) *Associate Councils with the World Council of Churches*

AUSTRALIAN COUNCIL OF CHURCHES
ÖKUMENISCHER RAT DER KIRCHEN IN ÖSTERREICH
BURMA CHRISTIAN COUNCIL
CANADIAN COUNCIL OF CHURCHES
NATIONAL CHRISTIAN COUNCIL OF CEYLON
ECUMENICAL COUNCIL OF CHURCHES IN CZECHOSLOVAKIA
ECUMENICAL COUNCIL OF DENMARK
ECUMENICAL COUNCIL OF FINLAND
ARBEITSGEMEINSCHAFT CHRISTLICHER KIRCHEN IN DEUTSCHLAND
HONG KONG CHRISTIAN COUNCIL
ECUMENICAL COUNCIL OF CHURCHES IN HUNGARY
NATIONAL CHRISTIAN COUNCIL OF INDIA
COUNCIL OF CHURCHES IN INDONESIA
NATIONAL CHRISTIAN COUNCIL OF JAPAN
COUNCIL OF CHURCHES IN MALAYSIA AND SINGAPORE
ECUMENICAL COUNCIL OF CHURCHES IN THE NETHERLANDS
NATIONAL COUNCIL OF CHURCHES IN NEW ZEALAND
NATIONAL COUNCIL OF CHURCHES IN THE PHILIPPINES

[20] Formerly the Union of Protestant Churches in the Netherlands Antilles.
[21] Formerly in membership through the United Methodist Church, U.S.A.
(q.v.).

POLISH ECUMENICAL COUNCIL
THE CHRISTIAN COUNCIL OF RHODESIA
SOUTH AFRICAN COUNCIL OF CHURCHES
SWEDISH ECUMENICAL COUNCIL
THE BRITISH COUNCIL OF CHURCHES
NATIONAL COUNCIL OF THE CHURCHES OF CHRIST IN THE USA
ECUMENICAL COUNCIL OF CHURCHES IN YUGOSLAVIA

(e) *National Organizations Affiliated to the Commission on World Mission and Evangelism*

FEDERACION ARGENTINE DE IGLESIAS EVANGELICAS
AUSTRALIAN COUNCIL OF CHURCHES[22]
ÖSTERREICHER MISSIONSRAT
MISSION PROTESTANTE DE BELGIQUE
CONFEDERACAO EVANGELICA DO BRASIL
BURMA CHRISTIAN COUNCIL[22]
CANADIAN COUNCIL OF CHURCHES[22]
NATIONAL CHRISTIAN COUNCIL OF CEYLON[22]
CONCILIO EVANGELICO DE CHILE
NATIONAL CHRISTIAN COUNCIL OF CHINA
CONSEJO CUBANO DE IGLESIAS EVANGELICAS
DANSK MISSIONSRAAD
FINNISH MISSIONARY COUNCIL
SOCIÉTÉ DES MISSIONS ÉVANGÉLIQUES DE PARIS
DEUTSCHER EVANGELISCHER MISSIONSRAT
THE CHRISTIAN COUNCIL OF GHANA
CONFERENCE OF MISSIONARY SOCIETIES IN GREAT BRITAIN AND IRELAND
HONG KONG CHRISTIAN COUNCIL[22]
NATIONAL CHRISTIAN COUNCIL OF INDIA[22]
COUNCIL OF CHURCHES IN INDONESIA[22]
JAMAICA COUNCIL OF CHURCHES
THE NATIONAL CHRISTIAN COUNCIL OF JAPAN[22]
NATIONAL COUNCIL OF CHURCHES IN KOREA
CHRISTIAN COUNCIL OF MADAGASCAR
CHRISTIAN COUNCIL OF MALAWI
COUNCIL OF CHURCHES OF MALAYSIA[22]
FEDERACION EVANGELICA DE MEXICO
NEAR EAST COUNCIL OF CHURCHES
NEDERLANDSE ZENDINGSRAAD
THE NATIONAL COUNCIL OF CHURCHES IN NEW ZEALAND[22]
EAST PAKISTAN CHRISTIAN COUNCIL
WEST PAKISTAN CHRISTIAN COUNCIL
NATIONAL COUNCIL OF CHURCHES IN THE PHILIPPINES[22]
CONCILIO EVANGELICO DE PUERTO RICO
CHRISTIAN COUNCIL OF RHODESIA[22]

[22] Associate Council of the World Council of Churches.

UNITED CHRISTIAN COUNCIL OF SIERRA LEONE
THE SOUTH AFRICAN COUNCIL OF CHURCHES[23]
SVENSKA MISSIONSRADET
CONSEIL SUISSE DES MISSIONS ÉVANGÉLIQUES
CHURCH OF CHRIST IN THAILAND
CHRISTIAN COUNCIL OF TRINIDAD AND TOBAGO
NATIONAL COUNCIL OF THE CHURCHES OF CHRIST IN THE U.S.A.[23]
FEDERACION DE IGLESIAS EVANGELICAS DEL URUGUAY
CHRISTIAN COUNCIL OF ZAMBIA

(f) Other Councils in Working Relationships with the World Council of Churches

BAHAMAS CHRISTIAN COUNCIL
FÉDÉRATION DES ÉGLISES PROTESTANTES DE BELGIQUE
CHRISTIAN COUNCIL OF BOTSWANA
BRITISH HONDURAS CHRISTIAN SOCIAL COUNCIL
ALLIANCE DES ÉGLISES PROTESTANTES DE BURUNDI
FÉDÉRATION DES ÉGLISES ET MISSIONS ÉVANGÉLIQUES DU CAMEROUN
ÉGLISE DU CHRIST AU CONGO
CURACAO COUNCIL OF CHURCHES
ETHIOPIA INTER-MISSION COUNCIL
FIJI COUNCIL OF CHURCHES
FÉDÉRATION PROTESTANTE DE FRANCE
ARBEITSGEMEINSCHAFT CHRISTLICHER KIRCHEN IN DER D.D.R.
GUYANA COUNCIL OF CHURCHES
IRAN COUNCIL OF CHURCHES
UNITED CHRISTIAN COUNCIL IN ISRAEL
IRISH COUNCIL OF CHURCHES
NATIONAL CHRISTIAN COUNCIL OF KENYA
CHRISTIAN COUNCIL OF LESOTHO
MELANESIAN COUNCIL OF CHURCHES
NEW HEBRIDES CHRISTIAN COUNCIL
CHRISTIAN COUNCIL OF NIGERIA
CONSEIL PROTESTANT DU RWANDA
CHRISTIAN COUNCIL OF ST. VINCENT
SCOTTISH CHURCHES COUNCIL
SUDAN COUNCIL OF CHURCHES
SWAZILAND CONFERENCE OF CHURCHES
CHRISTIAN COUNCIL OF TANZANIA
JOINT CHRISTIAN COUNCIL OF UGANDA
COUNCIL OF CHURCHES FOR WALES

[23] Associate Council of the World Council of Churches.

(g) *A Message from the Fourth Assembly of the World Council of Churches*[24]

The excitement of new scientific discoveries, the protest of student revolts, the shock of assassinations, the clash of wars: these mark the year 1968. In this climate the Uppsala Assembly met first of all to listen.

We heard the cry of those who long for peace; of the hungry and exploited who demand bread and justice; of the victims of discrimination who claim human dignity; and of the increasing millions who seek for the meaning of life.

God hears these cries and judges us. He also speaks the liberating Word. We hear him say—I go before you. Now that Christ carries away your sinful past, the Spirit frees you to live for others. Anticipate my Kingdom in joyful worship and daring acts. The Lord says, 'I make all things new'.

We ask you, trusting in God's renewing power, to join in these anticipations of God's Kingdom, showing now something of the newness which Christ will complete.

1. All men have become neighbours to one another. Torn by our diversities and tensions, we do not yet know how to live together. *But God makes new.* Christ wants his Church to foreshadow a renewed human community.

Therefore, we Christians will manifest our unity in Christ by entering into full fellowship with those of other races, classes, age, religious and political convictions, in the place where we live. Especially we shall seek to overcome racism wherever it appears.

2. Scientific discoveries and the revolutionary movements of our time open new potentialities and perils for men. Man is lost because he does not know who he is. *But God makes new.* The biblical message is that man is God's trustee for creation, that in Christ the 'new man' appears and demands decision.

Therefore, with our fellow-men we accept our trusteeship over creation, guarding, developing and sharing its resources. As Christians we proclaim Jesus as Lord and Saviour. God can transform us into Christ's new humanity.

3. The ever widening gap between the rich and the poor, fostered by armament expenditure, is the crucial point of decision today. *But God makes new.* He has made us see that Christians who in their acts deny dignity to their fellow men deny Jesus Christ, in spite of all that they profess to believe.

Therefore, with people of all convictions, we Christians want to ensure human rights in a just world community. We shall work for disarmament and for trade agreements fair to all. We are ready to tax ourselves in furtherance of a system of world taxation.

[24] The *Messages* of the previous Assemblies are printed in the author's earlier volume, *The Ecumenical Movement.*

4. These commitments demand the worship, discipline and mutual correction of a world-wide community. In the World Council of Churches, and its regional, national and local counterparts, only the beginning of this community has been given to us. *But God makes new.* The ecumenical movement must become bolder, and more representative. Our churches must acknowledge that this movement binds us to renewal.

Therefore, we re-affirm our covenant to support and correct one another. Present plans for church union call for decision, and we seek fuller communion with those churches which are not yet in full fellowship with us. We know that we never live the fullness of what we profess and we long for God to take over. Yet we rejoice that already we can anticipate in worship the time when God renews ourselves, all men, all things.

A Prayer

God, our Father, you can make all things new.
We commit ourselves to you: help us
— to live for others since love includes all men,
— to seek those truths which we have not yet seen,
— to obey your commands which we have heard but not yet obeyed,
— to trust each other in the fellowship which you have given to us;
and may we be renewed by your Spirit through Jesus Christ, your Son and our Lord. Amen.

(h) *Conciliarity and the future of the Ecumenical Movement*

Extracts from a statement of the Commission on Faith and Order, Louvain, Belgium, 1941.[25]

The Uppsala Assembly spoke of the World Council as a 'transitional opportunity for eventually actualising a truly universal, ecumenical, conciliar form of common life', and suggested that the member churches should 'work for the time when a genuinely universal council may once more speak for all Christians and lead the way into the future'. . . .

Conciliarity has been, in some form or degree, characteristic of the life of the Christian Church in all ages and at various levels. By conciliarity we mean the coming together of Christians—locally, regionally or globally—for common prayer, counsel and decision, in the belief that the Holy Spirit can use such meetings for his own purpose of reconciling, renewing and reforming the Church by guiding it towards the fullness of truth and love. Conciliarity can find different expressions at different times and places. The ecumenical movement has both challenged and helped us to seek appropriate conciliar forms for our own time. Facing the questions of the contemporary world, and drawn together by a common desire to serve the Lord together in the whole life and mission of the Church, the

[25] The full text of this statement appears in the *Ecumenical Review*, Vol. 24, no. 1, January 1972.

churches have been led in our own time to develop new forms of conciliarity—both within each church, and in councils of churches at the local, national, regional and world levels. It is important that we should reflect upon this fact, should endeavour to relate it to the conciliar experience of the Church in the past, and should seek more adequate forms of conciliarity for our day. . . .

The report of the Uppsala Assembly first calls for 'eventually actualising a truly ecumenical conciliar form of life' and then asks the churches to 'work towards the time when a genuinely universal council may once more speak for all Christians and lead the way into the future'. Though related, these two suggestions need to be distinguished. The first points to a permanent feature of the Church's life, while the second refers to an event which may once take place. To accept the first suggestion of the Uppsala Assembly will mean that we seek to deepen the element of conciliarity in the life of the churches at all levels, local, regional and universal. The New Delhi statement on the nature of the unity we seek spoke of a 'fully committed fellowship' both 'in each place' and also universally embracing the Church in all ages and places. To accept conciliarity as the direction in which we must move means deepening our mutual commitment at all levels. This does not mean movement in the direction of uniformity. On the contrary, our discussions here at Louvain have emphasized the fact, that, if the unity of the Church is to serve the unity of mankind, it must provide room both for wide variety of forms, and for differences and even conflicts. . . .

True conciliarity, moreover, has a temporal dimension; it links the past the present and the future in a single life. This is part of the meaning of what New Delhi said about the unity of one committed fellowship 'in all ages and all places'. Through the work of the Spirit in the life of the Church we are enabled to discern his teaching through the words of the councils of the past. Within the living fellowship of the one Church we are enabled to enter into a conversation with the past, to put questions and to receive illumination on our own problems. We are not called upon simply to reproduce the words of the ancient councils, which spoke to different situations and in languages other than ours. But it is an essential part of our growth into full conciliarity that we should be continually engaged in a process of 're-reception' of the councils of the past, through whose witness—received in living dialogue—the same Holy Spirit who spoke to the fathers in the past can lead us into His future.

The councils which have been created as expressions of the ecumenical movement in our time do not possess the fullness of conciliarity as it is to be seen in the great councils of the early Church. The reason of this deficiency is not in the first place their lack of universality. The central fact in true conciliarity is the active presence and work of the Holy Spirit. A council is a true council if the Holy Spirit directs and inspires it, even if it is not universal; and a universally representative body of Christians would not become a true council if the Spirit did not guide it. But the acceptance of a council as a true council in the full sense of the word implies that its decisions are accepted by the Church as fully authoritative, and that it has been marked by or has led to full eucharistic fellowship. However, the full acceptance of a council as authoritative has often taken a long period of time. It has not necessarily been the case that the complete binding authority of a council has been accepted in advance. We must therefore ask such questions as the following: What are the *pre*-conditions for a true council? Could there be a 'reunion council' which did not presuppose eucharistic fellowship and full consensus, but met seeking and expecting these as gifts of the Holy Spirit? These —as well as many other questions concerning the nature of representation, the role of bishops in a council, and other matters—require study. It is clear that the World Council of Churches and other similar regional and local councils are not in this full sense councils of the Church. They are meeting places for churches which are not yet in full communion and do not yet accept a common authority. They do nevertheless provide a framework within which true conciliarity can develop. In so far as they are guided and inspired by the Holy Spririt they have—if only in an anticipatory form—the character of conciliarity. . . .

We suggest that it will be by strengthening these elements of true conciliarity in the life of the World Council of Churches and its member churches that we shall move towards that 'fully committed fellowship' of which the New Delhi statement speaks. To accept this would mean at least the following:
(a) that all the member churches seek more earnestly to ensure that the ecumenical movement penetrates more and more fully into the life of local congregations, synods and assemblies of the churches;
(b) that member churches be encouraged to widen the area of organic unity and of eucharistic fellowship among them, wherever their fundamental ecclesiological principles permit;
(c) that the World Council of Churches explore still further the ways in which it can provide fellowship, support and guidance for those individuals and groups which are seeking new forms of Christian obedience for which existing ecclesiastical structures provide no opportunity;
(d) that the World Council be recognized as a place where the great issues on which Christians are divided may be faced—even at the risk of severe conflict, so that it may in a measure fufil the ancient function of a council as a place where Christians can be reconciled together in the truth;
(e) that member churches be encouraged to re-examine and (when appropriate and possible) interpret anew their polemical statements against each other;
(f) that the member churches together endeavour more seriously to achieve unity in faith and to confess together our hope for the world.

(i) *The Aims and Functions of the Programme Units of the Council.*[26]

PROGRAMME UNIT I — FAITH AND WITNESS

AIM

To seek God's will for the unity of the Church, to assist the churches to explore the content and meaning of the Gospel for their faith and mission, to encourage dialogue with men of other faiths and ideologies, and to enquire into the bearing of Christian belief on the spiritual and ethical issues posed for society by science and technology.

FUNCTIONS

(1) To gather the churches for common reflection on the content and meaning of the Gospel and the manner of its proclamation and witness.

(2) To proclaim the oneness of the Church and to keep prominently before the Council and the churches, within and outside its membership, the obligation to recover their unity in faith and worship.

(3) To promote and carry out biblical and theological studies on the nature of Christian life and witness as demand arises from the life of the member churches in their encounter with the contemporary world and from the concerns of the various branches of the ecumenical movement.

(4) To help churches and mission agencies to discern the opportunities and priorities for mission in different cultural and social circumstances; to encourage them to attempt new forms of mission and to plan and share their rescources for joint action in each place in such ways as will manifest more fully the unity of the Church.

(5) To study the theological implications of the existence and growth of the ecumenical movement and its varied manifestations and to cultivate relations with non-member churches and world confessional movements.

(6) To promote dialogue with men of living faiths including secular ideologies, and to help the churches to discern its implications for their life and for the understanding and communication of the Gospel in different situations.

(7) To promote interdisciplinary studies by groups of theologians, philosophers, scientists and others influencing the thought of men, to examine together the challenge to faith and human existence arising in modern science, philosophy and ideology, and to advise the churches on the ethical implications of such studies.

(8) To sponsor and undertake the initiation and administration of such programmes and agencies as may be required for carrying out the above functions.

[26] As adopted following the recommendations for the re-structuring of the Council (see above Chapter VII), and subject to revision before presentation to the Fifth Assembly in 1975.

PROGRAMME UNIT II — JUSTICE AND SERVICE

AIM

To assist the churches in promoting justice and peace in serving men through programmes designed to advance the dignity of man and the quality of the human community.

FUNCTIONS

(1) To mobilize the contribution of Christians and their churches towards a world community based on freedom, peace and justice.

(2) To promote ecumenical reflections and actions on the Christian responsibility in development, racism, international affairs and other issues in contemporary world society.

(3) To activate concern in the churches for the protection and implementation of human rights.

(4) To stimulate and assist Christian participation in the just resolution of international conflicts, and to promote the spirit of reconciliation and human solidarity in world affairs.

(5) To mobilize the churches in the world-wide struggle against racism; to express in word and deed solidarity with the racially oppressed and to aid the churches in educating their members for racial justice.

(6) To enable the churches to assist one another and to serve men in need, including the development of programmes to assist refugees, victims of war and natural disaster.

(7) To facilitate the transfer of resources, human and material, for projects and programmes in the field of development, social welfare and racial justice.

(8) To develop and coordinate the relationships of the World Council of Churches with governments and intergovernmental agencies, and other relevant organizations and movements.

(9) To help mobilize the whole people of God, irrespective of their organizational relationship to the World Council of Churches, in the fields of service, development, justice and peace.

PROGRAMME UNIT III — EDUCATION AND COMMUNICATION

AIM

To work with churches, councils and movements through processes of education and communication to enable persons, communities and institutions to participate as fully as possible in the changes that faith in God in Christ calls for in them, in churches, and in society.

FUNCTIONS

(1) To develop ways by which persons, groups and movements engaged in renewal may be mutually involved and supported for the benefit of the whole people of God.

(2) To study practices and theories of education, communication and processes of social change in the light of Christian experience, of theological thinking and of other relevant disciplines.

(3) To assist churches in developing programmes and stimulating in formal processes of Christian nurture of children, youth and adults, relevant to life in contemporary society.

(4) To improve the processes by which the relationships with and among the constituencies allow their diverse life and experience to contribute to one another, to the ecumenical movement and to the life of the World Council of Churches.

(5) To provide information and interpretation of the ecumenical movement and especially the World Council of Churches to the public at large and to the constituencies through inter-personal contacts, improved services of translations, printed materials, electronic media and the arts—with due consideration for the variety of cultures and languages.

(6) To develop working relationships, mutual aid and inter-change of information among the churches, their councils and agencies, which deepen their involvement in the determination, implementation and appraisal of ecumenical strategy.

(j) *The Structure of the World Council of Churches as reshaped in 1971*

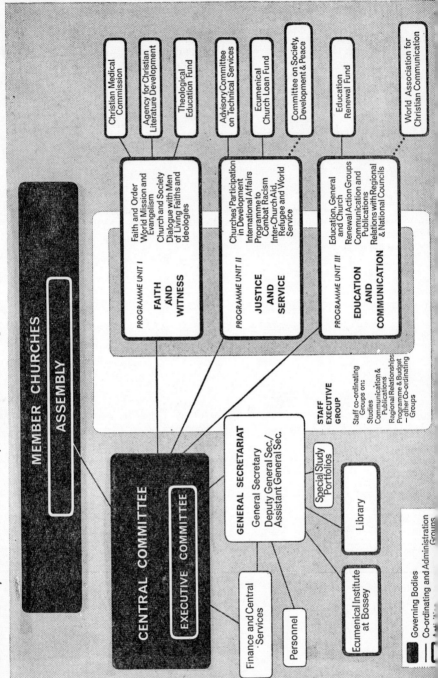

INDEX

Abbott, W. M., 127
Advisory Committee on Technical Services, *see* World Council of Churches
Africa, 5, 6, 28, 39, 46, 90; All Africa Conference of Churches, 105, 108f.; *Christian Ministry in Africa* (Sundkler), 90n.; independent churches, 109; literature needs, 97; medical services, 98; Organization for African Unity, 108; training of the ministry in, 89f.; WCC Emergency Fund, 109
Albania, 118
Amsterdam Assembly, *see* World Council of Churches
Ancient Oriental Churches, 65
Anderson, J. N. D., quoted, 38
Anglican Communion, 18, 65, 77; Consultative Council, 18; Executive Officer for, 18; Lambeth Conference, 18, 77
Angola, 56
Apartheid, 52f., 83, 86
Apostolicity and Authority, Joint R.C./WCC Study, 130
Argentina, 22, 116
Armenian Evangelical Union of Syria and Lebanon, 113
Asia, 5, 16, 46, 97f., 105f.; literature needs, 97; medical services, 98; training of the ministry in, 89. *See also* East Asia Christian Council
Associate Councils of WCC, 118, 158–9
Athenagoras I, Ecumenical Patriarch, 65
Australia, 111

Baillie, John, 59
Baldwin, James, 54
Bangalore Christian Institute for Study of Religion and Society, 31
Baptist Churches, attitude to Church Union, 76

Baptist Churches, Southern Conference of, U.S.A., 15
Baptist World Alliance, 18
Barnes, Roswell P., 2
Barry, David, quoted, 36
Barth, Karl, 59
Bea, Augustin Cardinal, 9
Beirut Conference on Development, 50f.
Beirut Conference on Refugee Problems, 45
Bell, George, 4
Biafra, 109
Black Power, 54, 55
Blake, Eugene Carson, ix–x, 50
Blauw, Johannes, 41
Boegner, Marc, 3, 60
Bossey, *see* Ecumenical Institute
Brazil, 22, 116
Brilioth, Ingve, 59
British and Foreign Bible Society, 97
British Council of Churches, 71, 119
Brunner, Emil, 59, 81
Buddhism, 27f.
Buganda, 39
Busia, K. A., 39

Canadian Council of Churches, 119
Caribbean, 5
Caribbean regional council, 119
Caritas Internationalis, 44, 128
Chile, 22, 90, 115, 116
Christian Aid, Great Britain, 103
Christian Approach to an International Ethos (C.C.I.A. study), 88
Christian Literature Fund (later Agency for Christian Literature Development), 97f., 103
Christian Medical Commission, 99f., 103
Christian Minister in India (Ranson), 89
Christian Ministry in Africa (Sundkler), 90n.
Christian Reconstruction in Europe, 43